# TEACHER'S PET PUBLICATIONS

LITPLAN TEACHER PACK
for
Pride and Prejudice
based on the book by
Jane Austen

Written by
Mary B. Collins

© 1996 Teacher's Pet Publications
All Rights Reserved

This **LitPlan** for Jane Austen's
Pride and Prejudice
has been brought to you by Teacher's Pet Publications, Inc.

Copyright Teacher's Pet Publications 1996

Only the student materials in this unit plan (such as worksheets,
study questions, and tests) may be reproduced multiple times
for use in the purchaser's classroom.

For any additional copyright questions,
contact Teacher's Pet Publications.

www.tpet.com

TABLE OF CONTENTS - *Pride and Prejudice*

Introduction	5
Unit Objectives	7
Reading Assignment Sheet	8
Unit Outline	9
Study Questions (Short Answer)	13
Quiz/Study Questions (Multiple Choice)	25
Pre-reading Vocabulary Worksheets	47
Lesson One (Introductory Lesson)	67
Nonfiction Assignment Sheet	69
Oral Reading Evaluation Form	71
Writing Assignment 1	74
Writing Assignment 2	85
Writing Assignment 3	87
Writing Evaluation Form	84
Vocabulary Review Activities	81
Extra Writing Assignments/Discussion ?s	79
Unit Review Activities	88
Unit Tests	91
Unit Resource Materials	123
Vocabulary Resource Materials	137

A FEW NOTES ABOUT THE AUTHOR
Jane Austen

AUSTEN, Jane (1775-1817). Through her portrayals of ordinary people in everyday life Jane Austen gave the genre of the novel its modern character. She began writing at an early age. At 15 she was writing plays and sketches for the amusement of her family, and by the time she was 21 she had begun to write novels that are among the finest in English literature.

Jane Austen was born on Dec. 16, 1775, in the parsonage of Steventon, a village in Hampshire, England. She had six brothers and one sister. Her father, the Rev. George Austen, was a rector of the village. Although she and her sister briefly attended several different schools, Jane was educated mainly by her father, who taught his own children and several pupils who boarded with the family.

Her father retired when Jane was 25. By that time her brothers, two of whom later became admirals, had careers and families of their own. Jane, her sister Cassandra, and their parents went to live in Bath. After the father's death in 1805, the family lived temporarily in Southampton before finally settling in Chawton.

All of Jane Austen's novels are love stories. However, neither Jane nor her sister ever married. There are hints of two or three romances in Jane's life, but little is known about them, for Cassandra destroyed all letters of a personal nature after Jane's death. The brothers had large families, and Jane was a favorite with her nephews and nieces.

Jane Austen wrote two novels before she was 22. These she later revised and published as 'Sense and Sensibility' (1811) and 'Pride and Prejudice' (1813). She completed her third novel, 'Northanger Abbey', when she was 27 or 28, but it did not appear in print until after her death. She wrote three more novels in her late 30's: 'Mansfield Park' (1814), 'Emma' (1816), and 'Persuasion' (published together with 'Northanger Abbey' in 1818).

She wrote of the world she knew. Her novels portray the lives of the gentry and clergy of rural England, and they take place in the country villages and neighborhoods, with an occasional visit to Bath and London. Her world was small, but she saw it clearly and portrayed it with wit and detachment. She described her writing as "the little bit (two inches wide) of ivory on which I work with so fine a brush, as produces little effect after much labor."

She died on July 18, 1817, after a long illness. She spent the last weeks of her life in Winchester, near her physician, and is buried in the cathedral there.

INTRODUCTION

This unit has been designed to develop students' reading, writing, thinking, and language skills through exercises and activities related to *Pride and Prejudice* by Jane Austen. It includes nineteen lessons, supported by extra resource materials.

The **introductory lesson** introduces students to the themes of pride and prejudice through a bulletin board activity. Following the introductory activity, students are given a transition to explain how the activity relates to the book they are about to read. Following the transition, students are given the materials they will be using during the unit. At the end of the lesson, students begin the pre-reading work for the first reading assignment.

The **reading assignments** are approximately thirty pages each; some are a little shorter while others are a little longer. Students have approximately 15 minutes of pre-reading work to do prior to each reading assignment. This pre-reading work involves reviewing the study questions for the assignment and doing some vocabulary work for 8 to 10 vocabulary words they will encounter in their reading.

The **study guide questions** are fact-based questions; students can find the answers to these questions right in the text. These questions come in two formats: short answer or multiple choice. The best use of these materials is probably to use the short answer version of the questions as study guides for students (since answers will be more complete), and to use the multiple choice version for occasional quizzes. It might be a good idea to make transparencies of your answer keys for the overhead projector.

The **vocabulary work** is intended to enrich students' vocabularies as well as to aid in the students' understanding of the book. Prior to each reading assignment, students will complete a two-part worksheet for approximately 8 to 10 vocabulary words in the upcoming reading assignment. Part I focuses on students' use of general knowledge and contextual clues by giving the sentence in which the word appears in the text. Students are then to write down what they think the words mean based on the words' usage. Part II nails down the definitions of the words by giving students dictionary definitions of the words and having students match the words to the correct definitions based on the words' contextual usage. Students should then have an understanding of the words when they meet them in the text.

After each reading assignment, students will go back and formulate answers for the study guide questions. Discussion of these questions serves as a **review** of the most important events and ideas presented in the reading assignments.

After students complete reading the work, there is a lesson devoted to the **extra discussion questions/writing assignments**. These questions focus on interpretation, critical analysis and personal response, employing a variety of thinking skills and adding to the students' understanding of the novel.

Following the discussion questions, there is a **vocabulary review** lesson which pulls together all of the fragmented vocabulary lists for the reading assignments and gives students a review of all of the words they have studied.

The **group activity** which follows the vocabulary lesson has students working in small groups to plan the wedding of Elizabeth and Darcy.

There are three **writing assignments** in this unit, each with the purpose of informing, persuading, or having students express personal opinions. The first assignment is to express personal opinions: students explain what they believe makes a successful relationship. The second assignment is to inform: following the group activity, students write a newspaper account of the wedding of Darcy and Elizabeth. The third assignment is to persuade: students think of a character or a real person who is prejudiced in some way and write a composition in which they persuade that person not to be prejudiced anymore.

In addition, there is a **nonfiction reading assignment**. Students are required to read a piece of nonfiction related in some way to *Pride and Prejudice*. After reading their nonfiction pieces, students will fill out a worksheet on which they answer questions regarding facts, interpretation, criticism, and personal opinions. During one class period, students make **oral presentations** about the nonfiction pieces they have read. This not only exposes all students to a wealth of information, it also gives students the opportunity to practice **public speaking**.

The **review lesson** pulls together all of the aspects of the unit. The teacher is given four or five choices of activities or games to use which all serve the same basic function of reviewing all of the information presented in the unit.

The **unit test** comes in two formats: multiple choice or short answer. As a convenience, two different tests for each format have been included.

There are additional **support materials** included with this unit. The **extra activities section** includes suggestions for an in-class library, crossword and word search puzzles related to the novel, and extra vocabulary worksheets. There is a list of **bulletin board ideas** which gives the teacher suggestions for bulletin boards to go along with this unit. In addition, there is a list of **extra class activities** the teacher could choose from to enhance the unit or as a substitution for an exercise the teacher might feel is inappropriate for his/her class. **Answer keys** are located directly after the **reproducible student materials** throughout the unit. The student materials may be reproduced for use in the teacher's classroom without infringement of copyrights. No other portion of this unit may be reproduced without the written consent of Teacher's Pet Publications, Inc.

UNIT OBJECTIVES - *Pride and Prejudice*

1. Through reading *Pride and Prejudice*, students will study the various facets of the trait of prejudice.

2. Students will study etiquette of a past era regarding courtship and marriage.

3. Students will compare and contrast characters to gain a better understanding of Jane Austen's portraits of human nature and to consider what characteristics are important to being a good person.

4. Students will demonstrate their understanding of the text on four levels: factual, interpretive, critical, and personal.

5. Students will define their own viewpoints on the aforementioned themes.

6. Students will be given the opportunity to practice reading aloud and silently to improve their skills in each area.

7. Students will answer questions to demonstrate their knowledge and understanding of the main events and characters in *Pride and Prejudice* as they relate to the author's theme development.

8. Students will enrich their vocabularies and improve their understanding of the novel through the vocabulary lessons prepared for use in conjunction with the novel.

9. The writing assignments in this unit are geared to several purposes:
   a. To have students demonstrate their abilities to inform, to persuade, or to express their own personal ideas
      NOTE: Students will demonstrate their ability to write effectively to <u>inform</u> by developing and organizing facts to convey information. Students will demonstrate the ability to write effectively to <u>persuade</u> by selecting and organizing relevant information, establishing an argumentative purpose, and by designing an appropriate strategy for an identified audience. Students will demonstrate the ability to write effectively to <u>express personal ideas</u> by selecting a form and its appropriate elements.
   b. To check the students' reading comprehension
   c. To make students think about the ideas presented by the novel
   d. To encourage logical thinking
   e. To provide an opportunity to practice good grammar and improve students' use of the English language.

READING ASSIGNMENT SHEET - *Pride and Prejudice*

Date Assigned	Chapters Assigned	Completion Date
	I: 1-9	
	I: 10-16	
	I: 17-23	
	II: 1-8	
	II: 9-13	
	II: 14-19	
	III: 1-5	
	III: 6-10	
	III: 11-19	

UNIT OUTLINE - *Pride and Prejudice*

1	2	3	4	5
Introduction PVR I:1-9	Study ?s I:1-9 PVR I:10-16	Study ?s I:10-16 PVR I:17-23	Study ?s I:17-23 PVR II:1-8	Study?s II:1-8 PVR II:9-13 PVR II:14-19
6 Writing Assignment 1	**7** Quiz/?s II:9-19 PVR III:1-5	**8** Library	**9** Study ?s III:1-5 PVR III:6-10	**10** Study ?s III:6-10 Nonfiction Reports PVR III:11-19
11 Study ?s III:11-19 Extra ?s	**12** Vocabulary	**13** Group Activity	**14** Group Activity	**15** Writing Assignment 2
16 Guest Speaker	**17** Writing Assignment #3	**18** Review	**19** Test	

Key: P = Preview Study Questions   V = Prereading Vocabulary Work   R = Read

10

STUDY GUIDE QUESTIONS

SHORT ANSWER STUDY GUIDE QUESTIONS - *Pride and Prejudice*

I:1-9
1. What does Mrs. Bennet wish Mr. Bennet to do?
2. What opinion does Mr. Bennet have of his daughters, with the exception of Lizzy?
3. What recommends Mr. Bingley to Mrs. Bennet?
4. Describe Mr. Bennet's character.
5. What kind of a young man is Mr. Bingley?
6. How does Mr. Darcy conduct himself at the ball?
7. Why doesn't Darcy ask Elizabeth to dance?
8. Describe the personalities of Elizabeth and Jane.
9. How does Charlotte excuse Darcy's pride?
10. Why does Charlotte say that Jane is too guarded in her feelings?
11. Why is Darcy intrigued and attracted by Elizabeth?
12. Although Mrs. Bennet is an unwise and foolish woman, why can we understand her pursuit of rich young men for her daughters?
13. Why won't Mrs. Bennet allow Jane to use the carriage to go to Netherfield?
14. Why does Elizabeth dislike Bingley's sisters?

I:10-16
1. Why is the exchange between Darcy and Miss Bingley amusing to Elizabeth?
2. During Darcy and Elizabeth's lively discussion, what character flaws do they attribute to each other?
3. Why does Mrs. Bennet refuse to send the carriage for Jane and Elizabeth?
4. Identify the speaker and the motive: "May I ask whether these pleasing attentions proceed from the impulse of the moment, or are the result of previous study?"
5. What is Mr. Collins' motive for visiting the Bennet family?
6. What passes between Darcy and Wickham?
7. What does Wickham relate to Elizabeth about his relationship with Darcy?
8. Identify the speaker, and explain Austen's inference: "A young man too, like you, whose very countenance may vouch for your being amiable."

I:17-23
1. How does Elizabeth's reaction to Wickham's distressing tale differ from Jane's?
2. Who has Mr. Collins decided will be his wife at this point in the novel?
3. What does Darcy say to Elizabeth concerning Wickham?
4. Why does Mr. Collins disregard Elizabeth's rejection of his marriage proposal?
5. What choice does Mr. Bennet offer Elizabeth concerning Mr. Collins' proposal?
6. Why would Charlotte agree to marry Mr. Collins, whom she does not love?

Pride and Prejudice Short Answer Study Questions Page 2

II:1-8
1. Identify the speaker: "The more I see of the world, the more I am dissatisfied with it; and everyday confirms my belief of the inconsistency of all human characters, and of the little dependence that can be placed on the appearance of either merit or sense."
2. What does Mrs. Gardiner suggest as a diversion for Jane?
3. Why does Mrs. Gardiner warn Elizabeth not to fall in love with Wickham?
4. Describe Elizabeth's double standard concerning Charlotte and Wickham.
5. How is Elizabeth to spend part of her summer?
6. Who says this, and why does she say it: "Yes, she will do for him very well. She will make him a proper wife"?
7. What kind of a woman is Lady Catherine De Bourgh?

II:9-13
1. What does the reader know and Charlotte begin to suspect at this point in the novel, regarding Darcy and Elizabeth?
2. What does Col. Fitzwilliam tell Elizabeth?
3. Why does Darcy's proposal make Elizabeth angry?
4. What excuse did Darcy give for separating Bingley and Jane?
5. What kind of a man does Darcy reveal Wickham to be?
6. What does Elizabeth realize about herself after reading Darcy's letter?

II:14-19
1. Why doesn't Elizabeth immediately tell Jane of Darcy's proposal?
2. Where does Mrs. Bennet want Mr. Bennet to take the family for the summer?
3. Do Jane and Elizabeth want to publicize Wickham's character? Why or why not?
4. How is Lydia able to go to Brighton?
5. Why does Elizabeth appeal to her father not to let Lydia go to Brighton?
6. Why does Mr. Bennet allow Lydia to go to Brighton?
7. What does Elizabeth find "reprehensible" about her father's behavior?
8. Where do the Gardiners take Elizabeth even though she is reluctant to go?

III:1-5
1. How do Darcy and Elizabeth react upon seeing each other at Pemberley?
2. What special attention and compliment does Darcy pay Elizabeth?
3. What does Elizabeth think of Georgiana?
4. How does Miss Bingley treat Elizabeth?
5. What do Lydia and Wickham do?
6. Although the elopement is distressing to the family, what gives them cause for more distress?
7. Where did Mr. Bennet go?
8. How does Mrs. Bennet react to the news of Lydia's elopement?
9. Is Lydia concerned about her flight and reputation?

Pride and Prejudice Short Answer Study Questions Page 3

III:6-10
1. What did Mr. Collins say in his letter regarding Lydia's situation?
2. Who finds Lydia and Wickham, and what is their state?
3. What arrangements were made so that the wedding could take place?
4. How does Mrs. Bennet react to the good news of Lydia's marriage?
5. What provision is made for the Wickhams?
6. Who is Elizabeth surprised to find out attended Lydia's wedding?
7. What does Mrs. Gardiner reveal to Elizabeth about Darcy's involvement in Lydia's marriage?
8. What was Darcy's motive for helping the Bennets?

III:11-19
1. Why is the call paid by Bingley and Darcy so awkward?
2. How does Jane profess to feel about Bingley? Why?
3. What happy event occurs between Jane and Bingley?
4. What does Lady Catherine demand of Elizabeth?
5. What plans has Lady Catherine already made for Darcy?
6. What is Elizabeth's answer to Lady Catherine?
7. What is the result of Lady Catherine's interference?
8. Why is Elizabeth apprehensive about communicating her engagement to Darcy?
9. What reason does Elizabeth offer Darcy to account for his beginning to love her?
10. How does Kitty benefit from her sisters' marriages?

ANSWER KEY: SHORT ANSWER STUDY GUIDE QUESTIONS - *Pride and Prejudice*

I:1-9

1. What does Mrs. Bennet wish Mr. Bennet to do?
    She wants him to call on the new occupant of Netherfield Hall so that their daughters may then make his acquaintance.

2. What opinion does Mr. Bennet have of his daughters, with the exception of Lizzy?
    He considers them silly and ignorant.

3. What recommends Mr. Bingley to Mrs. Bennet?
    He is a bachelor and has lots of money.

4. Describe Mr. Bennet's character.
    As a man surrounded by five daughters and a wife, he is obviously bored (or oppressed) by giddy female society. He entertains himself by teasing them and exercising his rather sarcastic wit upon them.

5. What kind of a young man is Mr. Bingley?
    He is a very pleasant man who seems fond of company and dancing.

6. How does Mr. Darcy conduct himself at the ball?
    He is very proud and formal and makes no effort to get to know anyone there or to dance with any strangers.

7. Why doesn't Darcy ask Elizabeth to dance?
    Darcy doesn't enjoy dancing unless he is already acquainted with his partner. Since he finds Elizabeth merely "tolerable," he rejects her.

8. Describe the personalities of Elizabeth and Jane.
    Jane is all goodness. She never speaks badly of anyone if at all possible. She is patient and gentle. Elizabeth has a sharper mind and tongue than Jane. She speaks her mind and holds independent views.

9. How does Charlotte excuse Darcy's pride?
    She says that since he has so much to be proud of--money, family connections, good looks--that he "has a right to be proud."

10. Why does Charlotte say that Jane is too guarded in her feelings?
    She asks Elizabeth how Mr. Bingley is ever to know of Jane's attachment to him if she conducts herself with so much composure. Charlotte argues that Mr. Bingley cannot see deeply into someone he has only just met, and that Jane had better make it plain that she is attracted to him, or he may think her indifferent.

11. Why is Darcy intrigued and attracted by Elizabeth?
    He thinks her eyes are "fine," her mind is quick, and he also is intrigued because she "would object to such a partner" as himself.

12. Although Mrs. Bennet is an unwise and foolish woman, why can we understand her pursuit of rich young men for her daughters?
    Mr. Bennet's estate is entailed on a distant male relation; therefore, his daughters will lose Longbourn upon his death. Mrs. Bennet wants to see her daughters with secure futures.

13. Why won't Mrs. Bennet allow Jane to use the carriage to go to Netherfield?
    Since it looks like it is going to rain, Mrs. Bennet wants Jane to go on horseback so she will have to spend at least one night there.

14. Why does Elizabeth dislike Bingley's sisters?
    She regards them as shallow snobs. They pretend affections towards Jane yet criticize her family and ignore her if it is to their own advantage. They clearly do not think Jane is an acceptable match for their brother even though they admit she is a nice girl.

I:10-16
1. Why is the exchange between Darcy and Miss Bingley amusing to Elizabeth?
    She is delighted that their dialogue confirms her opinion of them both: that Miss Bingley is a snob with her eye on Darcy and that Darcy is indifferent to Miss Bingley and is quite a rude man.

2. During Darcy and Elizabeth's lively discussion, what character flaws do they attribute to each other?
    She concludes that his "defect is a propensity to hate everybody," and he concludes that hers "is willfully to misunderstand them."

3. Why does Mrs. Bennet refuse to send the carriage for Jane and Elizabeth?
    She wants them to remain at Netherfield at least until the following Tuesday to increase Jane's chances of totally winning Bingley's heart.

4. Identify the speaker and the motive: "May I ask whether these pleasing attentions proceed from the impulse of the moment, or are the result of previous study?"
    Mr. Bennet is deriving great pleasure from his extremely ridiculous cousin. Mr. Collins is proud not only to pay Lady Catherine compliments but to spend time and effort composing them.

5. What is Mr. Collins' motive for visiting the Bennet family?
   He says he wants a better relationship with the Bennets. He wants to choose a wife from among the Bennet sisters so that at least one of the sisters can still claim Longbourn as the family home after Mr. Bennet's death.

6. What passes between Darcy and Wickham?
   The two men recognize each other yet barely acknowledge that fact. Elizabeth notices that the faces of both men color drastically, and she wonders why.

7. What does Wickham relate to Elizabeth about his relationship with Darcy?
   He says that they were boyhood friends but that Darcy grew to hate him because Wickham was a favorite of Mr. Darcy, Darcy's father. When it was Darcy's responsibility to ensure that Wickham was given a living, Darcy refused. So it is that Wickham has sought a commission instead of receiving his rightful inheritance.

8. Identify the speaker, and explain Austen's inference: "A young man too, like you, whose very countenance may vouch for your being amiable."
   Elizabeth considers how unfairly and cruelly Darcy has treated the handsome Wickham. Austen suggests with this line that Elizabeth is putting more weight on Wickham's looks than his word. This is one example of Elizabeth's inability to properly judge situations in which she is involved. She is usually very perceptive about everyone's business but her own.

I:17-23

1. How does Elizabeth's reaction to Wickham's distressing tale differ from Jane's?
   Elizabeth gets mad and despises Darcy. Jane considers that there must be some misunderstanding ("accident or mistake") to explain the situation.

2. Who has Mr. Collins decided will be his wife at this point in the novel?
   Seeing Jane's interests are elsewhere, he decides to give Elizabeth the honor.

3. What does Darcy say to Elizabeth concerning Wickham?
   He says that Wickham makes new friends with ease but that he doubts Wickham's ability to keep those friends.

4. Why does Mr. Collins disregard Elizabeth's rejection of his marriage proposal?
   First of all, it is beyond his comprehension that any woman, particularly one of Elizabeth's social standing, would reject his proposal. Secondly, he believes it is the practice of young ladies to reject proposals only as a flirtation, a method of keeping their intendeds in a state of suspense.

5. What choice does Mr. Bennet offer Elizabeth concerning Mr. Collins' proposal?
> He says that if she refuses Mr. Collins, her mother will not see her again, and that if she accepts him, her father will never see her again.

6. Why would Charlotte agree to marry Mr. Collins, whom she does not love?
> As she says herself, she is not a romantic person, and yet she must find a situation for herself. She regards her choice as a sound business decision.

II:1-8

1. Identify the speaker: "The more I see of the world, the more I am dissatisfied with it; and every day confirms my belief of the inconsistency of all human characters, and of the little dependence that can be placed on the appearance of either merit or sense."
> Elizabeth is speaking to Jane about how she has been disappointed concerning the characters of Charlotte and Bingley. (Consider this little speech in regard to the "dependence" Elizabeth places on "appearance" concerning Wickham and Darcy.)

2. What does Mrs. Gardiner suggest as a diversion for Jane?
> She suggests that Jane should accompany them back to London for a stay and to enjoy a change of scenery.

3. Why does Mrs. Gardiner warn Elizabeth not to fall in love with Wickham?
> Wickham has no money, and although he is charming and handsome, Mrs. Gardiner advises Elizabeth to be more prudent and responsible than to fall for an appealing picture. She reminds Elizabeth that a woman must use her good sense as well as her heart when considering a husband.

4. Describe Elizabeth's double standard concerning Charlotte and Wickham.
> She cannot understand Charlotte's marrying Mr. Collins solely for security, yet she finds Wickham's actions (of becoming interested in a young woman who recently acquired ten thousand pounds) perfectly normal for a young man without a fortune. She finds Wickham's decision to be wise and Charlotte's to be foolish.

5. How is Elizabeth to spend part of her summer?
> She will be traveling the country with the Gardiners.

6. Who says this, and why does she say it: "Yes, she will do for him very well. She will make him a proper wife."
> Elizabeth makes this comment when she first sees the daughter of Lady Catherine. She thinks the young lady looks "sickly and cross" and is pleased that this is who Darcy is meant to marry.

7. What kind of a woman is Lady Catherine De Bourgh?
    She is a very rich woman who has grown long accustomed to being paid deference. In other words, she is used to getting her own way in everything with little or no debate. She is full of pride and self-importance.

II:9-13

1. What does the reader know and Charlotte begin to suspect at this point in the novel, regarding Darcy and Elizabeth?
    The reader knows and Charlotte begins to suspect that Darcy is in love with Elizabeth.

2. What does Col. Fitzwilliam tell Elizabeth?
    He tells her that Darcy has recently saved a dear friend from a most unpromising marriage. From the hints he gives, Elizabeth realizes that Darcy has kept Bingley from Jane.

3. Why does Darcy's proposal make Elizabeth angry?
    Rather than explaining how and why he loves her, he explains all the arguments against his marrying her, reasons he has condescended to overcome to make his proposal. He speaks of the inferiority of her family connections, her lack of fortune, and her family's being so inferior to him socially.

4. What excuse did Darcy give for separating Bingley and Jane?
    After studying Jane and Bingley together, Darcy came to the conclusion that Jane was fond of his friend but that she was not in love with him. He did not want to see his friend attached to or hurt by a woman who did not appear to feel strongly about him.

5. What kind of a man does Darcy reveal Wickham to be?
    Wickham is revealed as a totally immoral character. He feels no responsibility toward his benefactor, the late Mr. Darcy, and he squanders all the chances he has been given to have a good living.

6. What does Elizabeth realize about herself after reading Darcy's letter?
    She realizes that she placed her trust in Wickham's good looks and easy sociability, forgetting completely about the impropriety of his disclosures and actions. A gentleman would never reveal the negative kind of information he told Elizabeth about Darcy to a stranger, as Elizabeth was to him. She is mortified that Wickham's attentions blinded her to his faults.

II:14-19

1. Why doesn't Elizabeth immediately tell Jane of Darcy's proposal?
    She does not want to reveal any information about Bingley, and she is afraid she may tell too much if she begins a discourse on what has occurred between herself and Darcy.

2. Where does Mrs. Bennet want Mr. Bennet to take the family for the summer?
   She wants Mr. Bennet to take the family to Brighton in pursuit of the officers.

3. Do Jane and Elizabeth want to publicize Wickham's character? Why or why not?
   No, they feel that since he will be gone to Brighton in two weeks, they could keep silent.

4. How is Lydia able to go to Brighton?
   She is invited by Colonel Forster's wife.

5. Why does Elizabeth appeal to her father not to let Lydia go to Brighton?
   She believes Lydia is too foolish and empty-headed to be allowed to be nearly on her own among so many young officers, even for a moment. Elizabeth argues that Mrs. Forster is too like Lydia to be a proper chaperon and that Lydia will surely bring censure, if not disgrace, upon the family by her flamboyant behavior.

6. Why does Mr. Bennet allow Lydia to go to Brighton?
   He believes that in a larger town with a larger number of ladies, Lydia may realize her own insignificance. He also believes that since she has no fortune, she will not be prey for any young fortune hunters.

7. What does Elizabeth find "reprehensible" about her father's behavior?
   She thinks that having married solely on the basis of physical attraction and engaging personality, her father grew quickly disappointed with a wife of little reason. His manner of condoling himself by the constant ridicule of his wife pains Elizabeth, and she feels he has been negligent in seeing that his daughters are brought up properly.

8. Where do the Gardiners take Elizabeth even though she is reluctant to go?
   They take her to Pemberley.

III:1-5
1. How do Darcy and Elizabeth react upon seeing each other at Pemberley?
   They are surprised and act awkward with each other. Darcy rallies his emotions first and proceeds to be friendly, kind, and generous to Elizabeth and the Gardiners. Elizabeth remains in a state of embarrassed confusion during their walk about the grounds yet is very pleased with Darcy's conduct.

2. What special attention and compliment does Darcy pay Elizabeth?
   He expresses his sister Georgiana's wish to meet her, which means he has spoken to his sister about Elizabeth with warm regards.

3. What does Elizabeth think of Georgiana?
   She finds her to be very shy and not at all proud as she had supposed her to be.

4. How does Miss Bingley treat Elizabeth?
   She is jealous that Elizabeth has Darcy's interest, and she seeks to ridicule her and her family by mentioning the militia. She wishes to remind Darcy of the lower social status of Elizabeth's family.

5. What do Lydia and Wickham do?
   They run off together, supposedly to elope.

6. Although the elopement is distressing to the family, what gives them cause for more distress?
   They have heard that Lydia and Wickham have apparently not yet married and that Wickham never intended to marry Lydia; they are just living together.

7. Where did Mr. Bennet go?
   He went to London to try to find Lydia and Wickham and set them straight.

8. How does Mrs. Bennet react to the news of Lydia's elopement?
   She retreats to her room, sick with worry. She blames everyone but herself for Lydia's situation. She cries and laments her own pitiful situation, having been disgraced by her daughter. She fears Mr. Bennet will be killed in a duel and Mr. Collins will evict her and the other girls. All of her concerns revolve around herself.

9. Is Lydia concerned about her flight and reputation?
   No, in fact she says, "What a good joke it will be!" in a letter to Mrs. Forster.

III:6-10

1. What did Mr. Collins say in his letter regarding Lydia's situation?
   He thinks it would have been better if Lydia had died. He also regrets the over-indulgent upbringing which Lydia received and which is partly responsible for her actions. He also mentions, with a great sigh of relief, that he could have been more closely connected with the family and their disgrace (but he fortunately wasn't). His advice is for the family to cast out Lydia and never see or speak to her again.

2. Who finds Lydia and Wickham, and what is their state?
   Mr. Gardiner apparently locates them and settles terms with Wickham so that the two can be married. It seems that Wickham apparently had no intentions of getting married.

3. What arrangements were made so that the wedding could take place?
   It seems that Mr. Gardiner had offered Wickham a large sum of money to get him to marry Lydia.

4. How does Mrs. Bennet react to the good news of Lydia's marriage?
   She is overjoyed and eager to buy Lydia wedding clothes and to see the now "dear" Wickham.

5. What provision is made for the Wickhams?
    He is to join the "regulars" and leave for the north shortly. Mr. Gardiner felt it would be better if they both started out in a new place among strangers.

6. Who is Elizabeth surprised to find out attended Lydia's wedding?
    She was surprised Darcy was there.

7. What does Mrs. Gardiner reveal to Elizabeth about Darcy's involvement in Lydia's marriage?
    She reveals that it was Darcy who actually located Lydia and Wickham and paid Wickham's debts. Darcy was also the one who got Wickham a position in the regulars. Darcy's only stipulation was that the Gardiners should take all the credit for his actions.

8. What was Darcy's motive for helping the Bennets?
    He felt responsible for not publicizing Wickham's true character and for not protecting innocent people from Wickham, but his overriding motive was his love for Elizabeth.

<u>III:11-19</u>
1. Why is the call paid by Bingley and Darcy so awkward?
    Both men are in love and unsure of the reception they will receive, and the ladies are equally self-conscious. Considering Mrs. Bennet's ridiculous and sometimes rude behavior, the situation could not be anything but unsatisfactory.

2. How does Jane profess to feel about Bingley? Why?
    She says that she is happy that they can meet and talk together as friends and that she is over any hopes of holding his greater affection. She is on her guard and doesn't want to be disappointed by assuming too much from his kind attentions.

3. What happy event occurs between Jane and Bingley?
    Bingley asks Jane to marry him, and she accepts.

4. What does Lady Catherine demand of Elizabeth?
    She wants to know if Elizabeth and Darcy are engaged, and she demands that Elizabeth will never marry Darcy.

5. What plans has Lady Catherine already made for Darcy?
    Darcy is supposed to marry her daughter and join the two family fortunes.

6. What is Elizabeth's answer to Lady Catherine?
    She refuses to make any promise to Lady Catherine. She insists that she will act in her own best interests and for her own happiness.

7. What is the result of Lady Catherine's interference?
   She unknowingly gives Darcy hope that Elizabeth thinks better of him than she used to. Darcy knows Elizabeth well enough to know that she would have told Lady Catherine exactly what she thought of him had she still held him in contempt. Elizabeth's refusal to Lady Catherine's demand gives Darcy reason to think that she may actually accept his proposal.

8. Why is Elizabeth apprehensive about communicating her engagement to Darcy?
   She knows she will have to convince everyone that she truly loves him and admires him. Since she was the one who was so outspoken in her dislike of him formerly, she realizes that she will have to undo all that she has said concerning him.

9. What reason does Elizabeth offer Darcy to account for his beginning to love her?
   She teases him that he had never met a lady who gave him so much trouble. That she was often impertinent and sometimes rude to him was a relief from the regular patronizing attentions he had received.

10. How does Kitty benefit from her sisters' marriages?
    Removed from Lydia's bad influence and placed in her other sisters' care, she improved in intellect, sense, and manners.

STUDY GUIDE/QUIZ QUESTIONS MULTIPLE CHOICE FORMAT - *Pride and Prejudice*

I: 1-9

1. What does Mrs. Bennet wish Mr. Bennet to do?
   A. She wants him to sell their country estate and move to the city.
   B. She wants him to call in the new occupant of Netherfield Hall so that their daughters may then make his acquaintance.
   C. She wants him to send the oldest two girls to Cambridge to get a good education.
   D. She wants him to take the family to Paris for a vacation.

2. What opinion does Mr. Bennet have of his daughters?
   A. He is fiercely devoted to all of them but favors Mary the most.
   B. He thinks Jane is the prettiest, Lydia the brightest, and the others are nothing special.
   C. He favors Kitty because she reminds him the most of his wife; he thinks the others are just average.
   D. He thinks all but Lizzie are silly and ignorant.

3. What recommends Mr. Bingley to Mrs. Bennet?
   A. He is a third cousin on her father's side.
   B. He belongs to the same church and has been recommended by the pastor.
   C. He is a bachelor and has lots of money.
   D. He is the most handsome man in the area and has a number of male cousins.

4. How does Mr. Bennet entertain himself?
   A. He teases his daughters and exercises his sarcastic wit upon them.
   B. He ignores his family entirely and spends most of his time in the city.
   C. He teaches his daughters the fine arts as well as hunting and fishing.
   D. He spends most of his time with his wife, and sees each of his daughters daily for a brief chat.

5. Which of the following statements does not describe Mr. Bingley?
   A. He is young.
   B. He is very pleasant.
   C. He is fond of dancing.
   D. He is an intellectual.

6. How does Mr. Darcy conduct himself at the ball?
   A. He is flirtatious with all of the ladies.
   B. He is proud and formal and makes no effort to get to know anyone.
   C. He is shy and spends most of his time walking in the garden.
   D. He is loud and boisterous, and makes improper remarks; no one likes him.

I: 1-9 - *Pride and Prejudice* Multiple Choice Study Questions Continued

7. Why doesn't Darcy ask Elizabeth to dance?
    A. He only dances with girls who are more than six inches shorter than he is, so that he will seem taller; Elizabeth is his equal in height.
    B. He had already promised Mr. Bingley's sister that he would only dance with her.
    C. He doesn't know Elizabeth, thinks her only tolerable, and doesn't want to get to know her.
    D. He does not know how to dance, but is ashamed to admit it, since all men of accomplishment are supposed to know how to dance.

8. Which of the Bennet daughters is being described? She is all goodness, never speaks badly of anyone, is patient and gentle.
    A. Jane
    B. Elizabeth
    C. Kitty
    D. Lydia

9. True or False: Mary is the most independent of the girls. She speaks her mind and holds independent views.
    A. True
    B. False

10. True or False: Charlotte excuses Darcy by saying that he has a lot to be proud of--money, family connections, and good looks.
    A. True
    B. False

11. What opinion does Charlotte have that she shares with Elizabeth?
    A. She says that Darcy is not to be trusted and will bring sorrow to any woman who becomes involved with him.
    B. She says that Jane should make her feelings about Mr. Bingley known or he may think her indifferent and become attracted to someone else.
    C. She says Jane is far too outspoken.
    D. She says Mrs. Bennet should be less reserved in expressing her opinions.

I: 1-9 - *Pride and Prejudice* Multiple Choice Study Questions Continued

12. True or False: Darcy rejects Elizabeth because she is too intelligent, and it makes him feel inferior.
    A. True
    B. False

13. Although Mrs. Bennet is an unwise and foolish woman, why can we understand her pursuit of rich young men for her daughters?
    A. She wants to make sure they get better husbands than she did. She thinks she can ease some of the pain of her own mistake by helping them.
    B. She made a promise to her dying mother that she would take care of her girls, and she is determined to fulfill her promise.
    C. Mr. Bennet's estate is entailed on a distant male relative; therefore, his daughters will lose their home upon his death. She wants them to have secure futures.
    D. A mother's success was based on the wealth of her daughters and the number of grandchildren she had. Since Mrs. Bennet is very conscious of social position, she wants to make sure that she is doing everything she can to assure herself of high social standing.

14. Why won't Mrs. Bennet allow Jane to use the carriage to go to Netherfield?
    A. She is afraid to drive it herself and won't let any of her daughters learn either.
    B. The carriage is old and shabby, and she doesn't want the Bingleys to see it.
    C. Mr. Bingley is using the horses for a hunting party.
    D. Since it looks like it is going to rain, Mrs. Bennet wants Jane to go on horseback so she will have to spend at least one night there.

15. How does Elizabeth feel about Bingley's sisters?
    A. She likes them better than her own sisters.
    B. She thinks they are attractive and interesting.
    C. She regards them as shallow snobs.
    D. She thinks they are detestable and unintelligent.

I: 10-16 - *Pride and Prejudice* Multiple Choice Study Questions

1. True or False: The exchange between Darcy and Mr. Bingley is amusing to Elizabeth.
    A. True
    B. False

2. During a conversation, Person A concludes that Person B's defect "is a propensity to hate everybody," and Person B concludes that Person A's defect "is willfully to misunderstand them." Who are the two speakers?
    A. Person A is Jane and Person B is Bingley.
    B. Person A is Mr. Bennet and Person B is Mrs. Bennet.
    C. Person A is Elizabeth and Person B is Darcy.
    D. Person A is Mrs. Hurst and Person B is Charlotte.

3. Why does Mrs. Bennet refuse to send the carriage for Jane and Elizabeth?
    A. She fears that they are contagious and doesn't want them around the other girls.
    B. She wants them to stay at Netherfield a few more days to increase the chances of Jane totally winning Mr. Bingley's heart.
    C. Mr. Bennet is using the carriage and she has no way of getting in touch with him.
    D. She is afraid Jane will have a relapse if she goes out in the rain. If she gets sick again, Bingley will think her a weak, sickly person and may lose his attraction for her.

4. Identify the speaker and the motive: "May I ask whether these pleasing attentions proceed from the impulse of the moment, or are the result of previous study?"
    A. Mr. Bingley's sister is questioning Jane about her intentions towards Mr. Bingley.
    B. Mrs. Bennet is returning Mr. Bennet's sarcasm with some of her own.
    C. Elizabeth is responding to the first civil comments Darcy has made to her.
    D. Mr. Bennet is ridiculing his cousin, Mr. Collins, for the time he spends complimenting Lady Catherine.

5. What is Mr. Collins' motive for visiting the Bennet family?
    A. He wants to check on Mr. Bennet's health.
    B. He wants to look over the estates since he is already planning to sell it when Mr. Bennet dies.
    C. He wants to choose a wife from among the Bennet sisters.
    D. He wants to withdraw his claim on the estate and leave it to Bennet's daughters.

6. True or False: Darcy and Wickham recognize each other and exchange tense words. Wickham looked like he was going to strike Darcy, so Darcy excused himself and left the room.
    A. True
    B. False

I: 10-16 - *Pride and Prejudice* Multiple Choice Study Questions Continued

7. Which is not one of the statements that Wickham relates to Elizabeth about his relationship with Darcy?
    A. They were boyhood friends.
    B. Darcy hated Wickham because Darcy's father favored him.
    C. Darcy's father left half of his fortune to Wickham. Darcy was contesting the move in court.
    D. Wickham had sought a commission instead of receiving his inheritance.

8. Identify the speaker, and explain Austen's inference: "A young man too, like you, whose very countenance may vouch for your being amiable."
    A. Elizablth is talking to Darcy, giving him a compliment.
    B. Darcy is talkng to Wickham, being sarcastic.
    C. Elizabeth is talking to Wickham, perhaps showing she puts more stock in his looks than his words.
    D. Darcy is talking to Bingley's. Austen infers that Darcy is jealous of Bingley's good looks and good nature.

I: 17-23 - *Pride and Prejudice* Multiple Choice Study Questions Continued

1. The other characters have different reactions to Wickham's tale. Who thinks there must be some misunderstanding to explain the situation?
    A. Mr. Bennet does.
    B. Jane does.
    C. Mr. Bingley.
    D. Elizabeth does.

2. Who has Mr. Collins decided will be his wife at this point in the novel?
    A. He has decided on Elizabeth.
    B. He has decided on Lydia.
    C. He has decided on Jane.
    D. He has decided on Kitty.

3. What does Darcy say to Elizabeth concerning Wickham?
    A. He says that Wickham is a cheat and a fraud..
    B. He says that Wickham has a violent streak and should be watched carefully.
    C. He says that Wickham is of low birth and has no right being among good society.
    D. He says that Wickham makes new friends with ease, but is not able to keep them.

4. How does Mr. Collins react to Miss Bennet's rejection of his marriage proposal?
    A. He is insulted and threatens to throw the family out of the house if she does not accept.
    B. He thinks she is doing it to be flirtatious. It is beyond his comprehension to think he would be rejected.
    C. He desperately wants to get married, so he offers to keep all of the other sisters in the house until they get married. He also offers to let Mrs. Bennet live there as long as she wishes.
    D. He cheerfully reminds her that she has four sisters, and one of them will be smart enough to marry him. He also insinuates that she will not be welcome in the house after he is the owner.

5. True or False: Mr. Bennet tells his daughter that if she refuses Mr. Collins, her mother will not see her again, and if she accepts him, her father will never see her again.
    A. True
    B. False

6. Who agreed to marry Mr. Collins?
    A. Mary did.
    B. Kitty did.
    C. Lydia did.
    D. Charlotte did.

II: 1-8 - *Pride and Prejudice* Multiple Choice Study Questions

1. Identify the speaker: "The more I see of the world, the more I am dissatisfied with it; and every day confirms my belief of the inconsistency of all human characters, and of the little dependence that can be placed on the appearance of either merit or sense."
    A. Mr. Collins is talking to Mr. Bennet.
    B. Darcy is talking to Bingley.
    C. Elizabeth is talking to Jane.
    D. Mrs. Bennet is talking to Mrs. Gardiner.

2. What does Mrs. Gardiner suggest as a diversion for Jane?
    A. She suggest that Jane go to France and study painting.
    B. She thinks Jane should take a position as a governess for a few years.
    C. She wants Jane to plan a ball and invite all of the eligible young men she knows.
    D. She invites Jane to go to London and stay with her for a while.

3. True or False: Mrs. Gardiner encourages Elizabeth to pursue her relationship with Wickham, saying a woman must always follow her heart.
    A. True
    B. False

4. True or False: Elizabeth has a double standard concerning Charlotte and Wickham. She cannot understand Charlotte's marrying for security, yet she finds Wickham's action (of becoming interested in a young woman who recently acquired money) as perfectly normal for a young man without a fortune.
    A. True
    B. False

5. How is Elizabeth to spend part of her summer?
    A. She will take a cruise on a steamer and go to all of the major ports in Europe.
    B. She will visit the museums in London.
    C. She will study with a private tutor.
    D. She will travel in the country with the Gardiners.

6. Who says this, and why does she say it: "Yes, she will do for him very well. She will make him a proper wife."
    A. Mrs. Gardiner says it about Charlotte Lucas and one of the young officers.
    B. Mrs. Bennet says it about Catherine and Mr. Collins.
    C. Elizabeth says it about Darcy and Lady Catherine's daughter.
    D. Mrs. Hurst says it about Jane and Mr. Bingley.

II: 1-8 - *Pride and Prejudice* Multiple Choice Study Questions Continued

7. Which of the following does not describe Lady Catherine De Bourgh?
    A. She is very rich.
    B. She is full of pride and self-importance.
    C. She is used to getting her own way in everything with little or no debate.
    D. She is very lavish in the gifts she gives to those she likes.

II: 9-13 - *Pride and Prejudice* Multiple Choice Study Questions

1. True or False: At this point in the story, Charlotte begins to suspect that Darcy is falling in love with Elizabeth.
    A. True
    B. False

2. What does colonel Fitzwilliam tell Elizabeth?
    A. He tells her that Wickham is in love with a charming, wealthy young woman.
    B. He tells her that the regiment will soon be moving to the north.
    C. He tells her that he is planning a ball to introduce his single officers to the young women in the area.
    D. He tells her that Darcy has recently saved a dear friend from a most unpromising marriage.

3. How does Elizabeth react to Darcy's proposal?
    A. She is surprised and pleased that he thinks so highly of her although she is not sure she is ready to get married.
    B. She is angry because of the way in which he proposes. He points out the reasons he has condescended to overcome to make the proposal.
    C. She is overjoyed, and they immediately begin making wedding arrangements.
    D. She is filled with regret and sorrow because she cannot return his love.

4. What excuse did Darcy give for separating Bingley and Jane?
    A. After studying them together, Darcy came to the conclusion that Jane was not in love with Bingley. He didn't want to see his friend get hurt.
    B. He believed that Lady Catherine's daughter was a better match with Bingley because she was rich and more suited temperamentally. Also, he wanted to make sure he would still have access to Bingley's friendship. He was afraid that if Bingley stayed at Netherfield Park, instead of moving back to the city, they wouldn't see as much of each other.
    C. He didn't think Bingley was worthy of Jane.
    D. He was angry with Elizabeth and wanted to get back at her. He knew that by upsetting Jane's relationship with Bingley, he would upset Elizabeth.

5. What kind of man does Darcy reveal Wickham to be?
    A. Wickham is revealed as a good person who has been unfairly treated and misjudged.
    B. Wickham is revealed as a totally immoral character who has squandered all of the chances he has been given.
    C. Wickham is revealed as a meek and devout man of good moral quality.
    D. Wickham is revealed as a strict military man who has a code of ethics, though no religious beliefs.

II: 9-13 - *Pride and Prejudice* Multiple Choice Study Questions Continued

6. What does Elizabeth realize after reading Darcy's letter?
    A. She realizes that Wickham was going to take advantage of her.
    B. She realizes that Darcy really is as snobbish and ill-tempered as she originally suspected.
    C. She realizes that she placed her trust on Wickham's good looks and easy sociability, forgetting completely about the impropriety of his disclosures and actions.
    D. She realizes that she is tired of thinking about men and about relationships in general. She decides she needs a rest.

II: 14-19 - *Pride and Prejudice* Multiple Choice Study Questions

1. True or False: Elizabeth doesn't tell Jane about Darcy's proposal because she doesn't want to accidentally reveal any information about Bingley while she is describing the meeting between herself and Darcy.
    A. True
    B. False

2. Where does Mrs. Bennet want Mr. Bennet to take the family for the summer?
    A. She wants to go to the coast of Spain for some clean air and sunshine.
    B. She wants to go to London so the girls can attend plays, go to museums, and be a part of the social life in the city.
    C. She wants to go to Scotland to acquaint the girls with relatives there.
    D. She wants to go to Brighton in pursuit of the officers.

3. Do Jane and Elizabeth want to publicize Wickham's character?
    A. Yes, they want to warn all of the single girls to stay away from him.
    B. No, they feel that since he is leaving in two weeks, they can keep silent.

4. How is Lydia able to go to Brighton?
    A. She is going to stay with Charlotte.
    B. She is going to travel around the country with a few friends.
    C. She is going to go to Brighton with Colonel Forster's wife.
    D. She is going to volunteer in a military hospital in London.

5. Why does Elizabeth appeal to her father not to let Lydia go to Brighton?
    A. Elizabeth thinks that Lydia is too foolish and empty-headed to be nearly on her own.
    B. Elizabeth is jealous; she thinks Lydia is after Darcy.
    C. Elizabeth feels that the oldest girls should have the first opportunities for summer activities and the younger girls should have to stay at home with their mother.
    D. She is afraid that the summer will be very expensive for her father. She thinks the money should be applied equally to all of their dowries, thus increasing their chances of better marriages.

6. Why does Mr. Bennet allow Lydia to go to Brighton?
    A. He is stubborn: he is doing it simply because the others are against it and he wants to assert himself as head of the family.
    B. He is tired of Lydia's complaining and wants to get rid of her for a while.
    C. She is his favorite daughter, and he will do anything she asks.
    D. He believes that when she is exposed to a place with a larger number of ladies, she will realize her own insignificance.

II: 14-19 - *Pride and Prejudice* Multiple Choice Study Questions Continued

7. Elizabeth finds many things about her father's behavior "reprehensible." Which of the following is not one of her objections?
    A. He married solely on the basis of physical attraction and engaging personality.
    B. He ridicules his wife to amuse himself.
    C. He spends too much time reading, instead of seeing to the affairs of the family.
    D. He has been negligent in seeing that his daughters are brought up properly.

8. Where do the Gardiners take Elizabeth even though she is reluctant to go?
    A. They take her to Netherfield Park.
    B. They take her to Brighton.
    C. They take her to Meryton.
    D. They take her to Pemberly.

III: 1-5 - *Pride and Prejudice* Multiple Choice Study Questions

1. True or False: When Elizabeth and Darcy see each other, they are surprised and act awkward with each other.
    A. True
    B. False

2. What special attention and compliment does Darcy pay Elizabeth?
    A. He tells her she is fine enough to be presented at Buckingham Palace.
    B. He tells her she has grown more beautiful than ever.
    C. He asks her to attend a ball with him, and he promises to dance exclusively with her.
    D. He expresses his sister's wish to meet her, which means he has spoken to his sister about Elizabeth with warm regards.

3. What does Elizabeth think of Georgianna?
    A. She thinks Georgianna is a snob like the others.
    B. She thinks Georgianna is shy and not as proud as she had supposed.
    C. She thinks Georgianna is just plain mean.
    D. She thinks Georgianna is much smarter than the others and a worthy friend.

4. True or False: Miss Bingley is jealous that Elizabeth has Darcy's interest, and seeks to ridicule her in front of him.
    A. True
    B. False

5. What do Lydia and Wickham do?
    A. Lydia and Wickham as for permission to get married.
    B. Lydia has a nervous breakdown and Wickham leaves her.
    C. Lydia and Wickham run off together, supposedly to elope.
    D. Wickham loses a large sum of money in a bad investment and Lydia gets a job.

6. True or False: The family is distressed to hear that Lydia and Wickham have split up, and Lydia is living by herself in an apartment.
    A. True
    B. False

7. Where did Mr. Bennet go?
    A. He went to Brighton to reprimand the colonel.
    B. He went to see Mr. Collins for spiritual guidance.
    C. He went to London to try to find Lydia and Wickham and set them straight.
    D. He went to Bath for a rest because his nerves were frayed.

III: 1-5 - *Pride and Prejudice* Multiple Choice Study Questions Continued

8. How does Mrs. Bennet react to the news of Lydia's elopement?
    A. She retreats to her room and laments about her own pitiful situation.
    B. She puts all of her faith in God and prays continually for guidance.
    C. She vows to help her daughter in any way possible. She offers a reward for information and makes arrangements to accompany her husband on his journey.
    D. She has a stroke and becomes paralyzed.

9. Is Lydia concerned about her actions and reputation?
    A. Yes, she is.
    B. No, she isn't.

III: 6-10 - *Pride and Prejudice* Multiple Choice Study Questions

1. Mr. Collins mentioned several things in his letter regarding Lydia's situation. Which of the following was not mentioned?
    A. He thinks it would have been better if Lydia had died.
    B. He regrets the over-indulgent upbringing Lydia had.
    C. He advises the family to cast her out and never speak to her again.
    D. He smugly reminds them that if she had accepted his offer she would not be in this difficult situation now.

2. Who finds Lydia and Wickham?
    A. Mr. Collins does.
    B. Mr. Gardiner does.
    C. Mr. Bennet does.
    D. Elizabeth does.

3. What arrangements are made concerning Lydia?
    A. The colonel arranges a marriage with one of his older single officers.
    B. She agrees to marry a distant cousin.
    C. Wickham is offered a large sum of money to marry her.
    D. She is forced to marry a colleague of Mr. Collins.

4. How does Mrs. Bennet react to the news about Lydia's marriage?
    A. She is overjoyed and eager to buy Lydia wedding clothes and greet her "dear" husband.
    B. She is embarrassed and disappointed and refuses to acknowledge Lydia and her husband.
    C. She faints from the shock and relief.
    D. She packs her bags immediately to go to see Lydia.

5. What provision is made for Lydia and her husband?
    A. They are sent to live in the north to start out in a new place among strangers.
    B. They move to Australia.
    C. They move in with the Bennets temporarily.
    D. They are set up in a flat in London so that they can be watched over carefully.

6. Who is Elizabeth surprised to find out attended Lydia's wedding?
    A. She is surprised to find out that her father attended.
    B. She is surprised to find out that Darcy attended.
    C. She is surprised to find out that Lady Catherine attended.
    D. She is surprised to find out that Charlotte and Mr. Collins attended.

III: 6-10 - *Pride and Prejudice* Multiple Choice Study Questions Continued

7. True or False: Darcy reveals to Elizabeth that he was the one who actually located Lydia and arranged for her welfare and insisted that the Gardiners take the credit.
    A. True
    B. False

8. True or False: Darcy's overriding motive for helping the Bennets was his love for Elizabeth.
    A. True
    B. False

III: 11-19 - *Pride and Prejudice* Multiple Choice Study Questions

1. Which of the following terms describes the call paid by Darcy and Bingley?
    A. It was highly successful.
    B. It was awkward.
    C. It was tense and strained.
    D. It was calm and low-key.

2. True or False: Jane says that she is happy that she and Bingley can meet as friends and talk together and that she is over any hopes of holding his greater affection.
    A. True
    B. False

3. What occurs between Jane and Bingley?
    A. He proposes, and she accepts.
    B. He proposes, and she refuses.
    C. They both agree to part as friends.
    D. They part on unfriendly terms and agree never to speak to one another again.

4. What does Lady Catherine demand of Elizabeth?
    A. She demands that Elizabeth go to school and get a proper education so that she can be a better wife.
    B. She demands that Elizabeth travel around the continent for two years before she settles down.
    C. She demands that Elizabeth will never marry Darcy.
    D. She demands that Elizabeth allow her first-born daughter to be raised by Lady Catherine so that she is "brought up properly."

5. What plans has Lady Catherine already made for Darcy?
    A. She wants him to go into politics and join the House of Lords.
    B. She wants him to marry her daughter and join the family fortunes.
    C. She wants him to accompany her on several short vacations.
    D. She wants him to manage her business affairs.

6. What answer does Elizabeth give to Lady Catherine?
    A. She agrees to Lady Catherine's demands because she is afraid of getting Lady Catherine angry.
    B. She refuses to promise anything. She insists that she will act in her own best interests.
    C. She tells Lady Catherine, "You are a contemptuous, aristocratic snob, and I deplore the earth upon which you walk. Your demands are unworthy of any response, you spoiled, demanding wretch." And then she saunters out of the room.
    D. She agrees because she wants to please Lady Catherine.

III: 11-19 - *Pride and Prejudice* Multiple Choice Study Questions Continued

8. What is the result of Lady Catherine's interference?
    A. She unknowingly gives Darcy hope that Elizabeth thinks better of him than she used to.
    B. She drives an insurmountable wedge between Elizabeth and Darcy.
    C. She loses Darcy's respect and affection. He says he will never speak to her again.
    D. She creates a firm friendship between her daughter and Elizabeth.

9. How does Elizabeth feel about communicating her engagement to Darcy?
    A. She is smug and very satisfied with herself that she has conquered him.
    B. She realizes that she will have to convince everyone that she truly loves and admires him since she disliked him previously.
    C. She prefers to keep it a secret since Darcy isn't liked by most people.
    D. She doesn't want to tell anyone for a while because she might change her mind.

10. What reason does Elizabeth offer Darcy to account for his beginning to love her?
    A. She teases him that he had never met another lady who gave him so much trouble.
    B. She thinks she reminds him of his mother, for whom he has grieved for many years.
    C. He knows she is very practical and will not squander his fortune.
    D. He finally realizes that a man does not need to feel threatened by a woman's superior intellect.

11. How does Kitty benefit from her sister's marriages?
    A. She gets more attention from her parents.
    B. Removed from Lydia's bad influence and placed in her sisters' care, she improves in intellect, sense, and manners.
    C. She meets more eligible bachelors who are friends of her sisters' husbands.
    D. Mrs. Bennet is so busy doting on her sons-in-law that Kitty is free to do as she pleases.

ANSWER KEY: MULTIPLE CHOICE STUDY QUESTIONS - *Pride and Prejudice*

	I 1-9	I 10-16	I 17-23	II 1-8	II 9-13	II 14-19	III 1-5	III 6-10	III 11-19
1.	B	A	B	C	A	A	A	D	B
2.	D	C	A	D	D	D	D	B	B
3.	C	B	D	B	B	B	B	C	A
4.	A	D	B	A	A	C	A	A	C
5.	D	C	A	D	B	A	C	A	B
6.	B	B	D	C	C	D	B	B	B
7.	C	C		D		C	C	B	A
8.	A	C				D	A	A	B
9.	B						B		A
10.	A								B
11.	B								
12.	B								
13.	C								
14.	D								
15.	C								
16									

PREREADING VOCABULARY WORKSHEETS

VOCABULARY - *Pride and Prejudice*

<u>Volume I Chapters 1-9</u> Part I: Using Prior Knowledge and Contextual Clues

Below are the sentences in which the vocabulary words appear in the text. Read the sentence. Use any clues you can find in the sentence combined with your prior knowledge, and write what you think the underlined words mean on the lines provided.

1. Mr. Bennet was so odd a mixture of quick parts, sarcastic humour, reserve, and <u>caprice</u>, that the experience of three and twenty years had been insufficient to make his wife understand his character.

   _____

2. I honour your <u>circumspection</u>. A fortnight's acquaintance is certainly very little.

   _____

3. The ladies were somewhat more fortunate, for they had the advantage of <u>ascertaining</u> from an upper window, that he wore a blue coat and rode a black horse.

   _____

4. " I would not be so <u>fastidious</u> as you are," cried Bingley, "for a kingdom! Upon my honour, I never met with so many pleasant girls in my life, as I have this evening. . . ."

   _____

5. Elizabeth listened in silence, but was not convinced . . . with more quickness of observation and less <u>pliancy</u> of temper than her sister . . . . she was very little disposed to approve them.

   _____

6. For though elated by his rank, it did not render him <u>supercilious</u>; on the contrary, he was all attention to every body.

   _____

7. . . . and it has the advantage also of being in <u>vogue</u> amongst the less polished societies of the world.--Every savage can dance.

   _____

47

Vocabulary - *Pride and Prejudice* Volume I Chapters 1-9 Continued

8. Whatever bears <u>affinity</u> to cunning is despicable.

_____

9. I wonder who first discovered the <u>efficacy</u> of poetry in driving away love!

_____

Part II: Determining the Meaning: Match the vocabulary words to their dictionary definitions.

___ 1. caprice   A. discovering
___ 2. circumspection   B. haughty; disdainful
___ 3. ascertaining   C. effectiveness
___ 4. fastidious   D. impulsive change of mind
___ 5. pliancy   E. meticulous; difficult to please
___ 6. supercilious   F. prudence
___ 7. vogue   G. a natural attraction to
___ 8. affinity   H. flexibility
___ 9. efficacy   I. fashion; popularity

Vocabulary - *Pride and Prejudice* Volume I Chapters 10-16

Part I: Using Prior Knowledge and Contextual Clues

Below are the sentences in which the vocabulary words appear in the text. Read the sentence. Use any clues you can find in the sentence combined with your prior knowledge, and write what you think the underlined words mean on the lines provided.

1. Miss Bingley moved with alacrity to the piano-forte, and after a polite request that Elizabeth would lead the way, which the other as politely and more earnestly negatived, she seated herself.

   _____

2. Implacable resentment *is* a shade in a character.

   _____

3. Her answer, therefore, was not propitious, at least not to Elizabeth's wishes, for she was impatient to get home.

   _____

4. You are very kind, sir, I am sure; and I wish with all my heart it may prove so; for else they will be destitute enough. Things are settled so oddly.

   _____

5. Lady Catherine was reckoned proud by many people he knew, but *he* had never seen any thing but affability in her.

   _____

6. Mr. Denny and Mr. Wickham walked with the young ladies to the door of Mr. Philips's house, and then made their bows, in spite of Miss Lydia's pressing entreaties that they would come in . . .

   _____

7. . . . Mr. Darcy chose to doubt it . . . and to assert that I had forfeited all claim to it by extravagance, imprudence, in short any thing or nothing.

   _____

Vocabulary - *Pride and Prejudice* Volume I Chapters 10-16 Continued

8. I have not seen her for many years, but I very well remember that I never liked her, and that her manners were dictatorial and <u>insolent</u>.

_____

Part II: Determining the Meaning: Match the vocabulary words to their dictionary definitions.

   ___ 1. alacrity   A. pleas
   ___ 2. implacable   B. insulting; disrespectful; rude
   ___ 3. propitious   C. cheerful willingness
   ___ 4. destitute   D. quality of being pleasant & easy to speak to
   ___ 5. affability   E. impossible to appease or please
   ___ 6. entreaties   F. characteristic of making unwise decisions
   ___ 7. imprudence   G. favorable
   ___ 8. insolent   H. lacking; poor

Vocabulary - *Pride and Prejudice* Volume I Chapters 17-23
Part I: Using Prior Knowledge and Contextual Clues

Below are the sentences in which the vocabulary words appear in the text. Read the sentence. Use any clues you can find in the sentence combined with your prior knowledge, and write what you think the underlined words mean on the lines provided.

1. . . . it was not in her nature to question the <u>veracity</u> of a young man of such amiable appearance as Wickham.

_____

2. We are each of an unsocial, <u>taciturn</u> disposition, unwilling to speak, unless we expect to say something that will amaze the whole room . . . .

_____

3. It is particularly <u>incumbent</u> on those who never change their opinion, to be secure of judging properly at first.

_____

4. . . . he must make such an agreement for <u>tithes</u> as may be beneficial to himself and not offensive to his patron.

_____

5. Her daughters listened in silence to this <u>effusion</u>, sensible that any attempt to reason with or soothe her would only increase the irritation.

_____

6. He was anxious to avoid the notice of his cousins, from a conviction that if they saw him depart, they could not fail to <u>conjecture</u> his design, and he was not willing to have the attempt known till its success could be known likewise. . . .

_____

7. Her disappointment in Charlotte made her turn with fonder regard to her sister, of whose <u>rectitude</u> and delicacy she was sure her opinion could never be shaken . . . .

_____

Vocabulary - *Pride and Prejudice* Volume I Chapters 17-23 Continued

Part II: Determining the Meaning: Match the vocabulary words to their definitions.

___ 1. veracity   A. moral uprightness
___ 2. taciturn   B. money given to support the clergy
___ 3. incumbent   C. not talkative
___ 4. tithes   D. guess
___ 5. effusion   E. truthfulness
___ 6. conjecture   F. imposed as a duty or obligation
___ 7. rectitude   G. unrestrained outpouring of speech

Vocabulary - *Pride and Prejudice* Volume II Chapters 1-8

Part I: Using Prior Knowledge and Contextual Clues
    Below are the sentences in which the vocabulary words appear in the text. Read the sentence. Use any clues you can find in the sentence combined with your prior knowledge, and write what you think the underlined words mean on the lines provided.

1. Thoughtlessness, want of attention to other people's feelings, and the want of resolution, will do the business. And do you <u>impute</u> it to either of those?

_____

2. Mrs. Bennet still continued to wonder and <u>repine</u> at his returning no more . . . .

_____

3. But, my dear Elizabeth, . . . what sort of girl is Miss King? I should be sorry to think our friend <u>mercenary</u>.

_____

4. . . . he welcomed them a second time with <u>ostentatious</u> formality to his humble abode . . . .

_____

5. The subject was <u>pursued</u> no farther, and the gentlemen soon afterwards went away.

_____

6. . . . she was, in fact, almost <u>engrossed</u> by her nephews, speaking to them, especially to Darcy, much more than to any other person in the room.

_____

Vocabulary - *Pride and Prejudice* Volume II Chapters 1-8 Continued

Part II: Determining the Meaning: Match the vocabulary words to their dictionary definitions.

___ 1. impute   A. totally occupied
___ 2. repine   B. credit
___ 3. mercenary   C. advanced; chased after
___ 4. ostentatious   D. motivated by money or material gain
___ 5. pursued   E. to be discontented or in low spirits
___ 6. engrossed   F. pretentious; pompous

Vocabulary - *Pride and Prejudice* Volume II Chapters 9-13

Part I: Using Prior Knowledge and Contextual Clues
   Below are the sentences in which the vocabulary words appear in the text. Read the sentence. Use any clues you can find in the sentence combined with your prior knowledge, and write what you think the underlined words mean on the lines provided.

1. . . . she thought it not unlikely to be Lady Catherine, and under that apprehension was putting away her half-finished letter that she might escape all <u>impertinent</u> questions . . . .

_____

2. You need not be frightened. I never heard any harm of her; and I dare say she is one of the most <u>tractable</u> creatures in the world.

_____

3. You dare not, you cannot deny that you have been the principal, if not the only means of dividing them from each other, of exposing one to the censure of the world for caprice and instability, the other to its <u>derision</u> for disappointed hopes, and involving them both in misery of the acutest kind.

_____

4. But I shall not <u>scruple</u> to assert, that the serenity of your sister's countenance and air was such, as might have given the most acute observer, a conviction that, however amiable her temper, her heart was not likely to be easily touched.

_____

5. . . . he hoped I should not think it unreasonable for him to expect some more immediate <u>pecuniary</u> advantage, in lieu of the preferment, by which he could not be benefited.

_____

6. . . . his style was not <u>penitent</u>, but haughty.

_____

Vocabulary - *Pride and Prejudice* Volume II Chapters 9-13 Continued

Part II: Determining the Meaning: Match the vocabulary words to their dictionary definitions.

___ 1. impertinent A. ridicule
___ 2. tractable B. showing regret or remorse
___ 3. derision C. manageable; easily handled
___ 4. scruple D. relating to money
___ 5. pecuniary E. hesitate as a result of conscience
___ 6. penitent F. improperly bold or forward

Vocabulary - *Pride and Prejudice* Volume II Chapters 14-19

Part I: Using Prior Knowledge and Contextual Clues
　　Below are the sentences in which the vocabulary words appear in the text. Read the sentence. Use any clues you can find in the sentence combined with your prior knowledge, and write what you think the underlined words mean.

1. . . . and Mr. Collins having been in waiting near the lodges, to make them his parting obeisance, was able to bring home the pleasing intelligence of their appearing in very good health

_____

2. Their first subject was the diminution of the Rosings' party.

_____

3. Wholly inattentive to her sister's feelings, Lydia flew about the house in restless ecstasy, calling for every one's congratulations . . . .

_____

4. Had Lydia and her mother know the substance of her conference with her father, their indignation would hardly have found expression in their united volubility.

_____

5. Mrs. Bennet was diffuse in her good wishes for the felicity of her daughter, and impressive in her injunctions that she would not miss the opportunity of enjoying herself as much as possible. . .

_____

6. Had Elizabeth's opinion been all drawn from her own family, she could not have formed a very pleasing picture of conjugal felicity or domestic comfort.

_____

7. Mrs. Bennet was restored to her usual querulous serenity . . . .

_____

Vocabulary - *Pride and Prejudice* Volume II Chapters 14-19 Continued

8. Mr. Gardiner declared his willingness, and Elizabeth was applied to for her <u>approbation</u>.

_____

Part II: Determining the Meaning: Match the vocabulary words to their dictionary definitions.

___ 1. obeisance   A. fluency of speech
___ 2. diminution   B. a gesture of deference or homage
___ 3. ecstasy   C. relating to marriage
___ 4. volubility   D. approval
___ 5. injunctions   E. reduction
___ 6. conjugal   F. grumbling; complaining
___ 7. querulous   G. intense joy
___ 8. approbation   H. commands; orders

Vocabulary - *Pride and Prejudice* Volume III Chapters 1-5

Part I: Using Prior Knowledge and Contextual Clues
   Below are the sentences in which the vocabulary words appear in the text. Read the sentence. Use any clues you can find in the sentence combined with your prior knowledge, and write what you think the underlined words mean on the lines provided.

1. His acquaintance with Elizabeth was very trifling.

_____

2. She answered with equal indifference and brevity, and the other said no more.

_____

3. We both know that he has been profligate in every sense of the word.

_____

4. The sanguine hope of good, however, which the benevolence of her heart suggested, had not yet deserted her. . . .

_____

5. Mrs. Bennet . . . received them exactly as might be expected; with tears and lamentations of regret, invectives against the villainous conduct of Wickham . . . .

_____

Part II: Determining the Meaning: Match the vocabulary words to their dictionary definitions.

___ 1. trifling   A. cheerfully confident; optimistic
___ 2. brevity   B. wasteful; extravagant
___ 3. profligate   C. abusive language
___ 4. sanguine   D. of little significance
___ 5. invectives   E. quality of being short in duration; shortness

Vocabulary - *Pride and Prejudice* Volume III Chapters 6-10

Part I: Using Prior Knowledge and Contextual Clues
    Below are the sentences in which the vocabulary words appear in the text. Read the sentence. Use any clues you can find in the sentence combined with your prior knowledge, and write what you think the underlined words mean on the lines provided.

1. His family knew him to be on all common occasions, a most negligent and <u>dilatory</u> correspondent . . . .

_____

2. And this consideration leads me moreover to reflect with <u>augmented</u> satisfaction on a certain event of last November . . . .

_____

3. Another day I will do the same; I will sit in my library, in my night cap and powdering gown, and give as much trouble as I can,--or, perhaps, I may <u>defer</u> it, till Kitty runs away.

_____

4. If you are looking for my master, ma'am, he is walking towards the little <u>copse</u>.

_____

5. The kindness of my uncle and aunt can never be <u>requited</u>.

_____

6. That his anger could be carried to such a point of inconceivable resentment, as to refuse his daughter a privilege, without which her marriage would scarcely seem <u>valid</u>, exceeded all that she could believe possible.

_____

7. I am sure all my sisters must <u>envy</u> me. I only hope they may have half my good luck.

_____

Vocabulary - *Pride and Prejudice* Volume III Chapters 6-10 Continued

8. Pray write instantly, and let me understand it--unless it is, for very <u>cogent</u> reasons, to remain in the secrecy which Lydia seems to think necessary. . . .

_____

9. The <u>vague</u> and unsettled suspicions which uncertainty had produced of what Mr. Darcy might have been doing to forward her sister's match . . . .

_____

Part II: Determining the Meaning: Match the vocabulary words to their dictionary definitions.

___ 1. dilatory   A. convincing
___ 2. augmented   B. repaid
___ 3. defer   C. legal and binding
___ 4. copse   D. tending to delay
___ 5. requited   E. postpone
___ 6. valid   F. added
___ 7. envy   G. have a feeling of discontent aroused by a desire for the
                                      possessions or qualities of others
___ 8. cogent   H. unclear; not well-defined
___ 9. vague   I. thicket of small trees

Vocabulary - *Pride and Prejudice* Volume III Chapters 11-19

Part I: Using Prior Knowledge and Contextual Clues

Below are the sentences in which the vocabulary words appear in the text. Read the sentence. Use any clues you can find in the sentence combined with your prior knowledge, and write what you think the underlined words mean on the lines provided.

1. I could see him with perfect indifference, but I can hardly bear to hear it thus perpetually talked of.

_____

2. I am sure he will be vastly happy to oblige you, and will save all the best of the cavies for you.

_____

3. This naturally introduced a panegyric from Jane on his diffidence, and the little value he put on his own good qualities.

_____

4. This match to which you have the presumption to aspire, can never take place.

_____

5. Do you pay no regard to the wishes of his friends? To his tacit engagement with Miss De Bourgh?

_____

6. Young ladies have great penetration in such matters as these; but I think I may defy even *your* sagacity to discover the name of your admirer.

_____

7. *Your* retrospections must be so totally void of reproach, that the contentment arising from them, is not of philosophy, but what is much better, of ignorance.

_____

8. This was a sad omen of what her mother's behavior to the gentleman himself might be . . . .

_____

Vocabulary - *Pride and Prejudice* Volume III Chapters 11-19 Continued

Part II: Determining the Meaning: Match the vocabulary words to their dictionary definitions.

___ 1. perpetually   A. a prophetic sign
___ 2. oblige   B. empty
___ 3. panegyric   C. continually; constantly
___ 4. aspire   D. implied by actions
___ 5. tacit   E. wisdom; judgement
___ 6. sagacity   F. do a favor or service for
___ 7. void   G. desire; to have as an ambition or a goal
___ 8. omen   H. praise; compliment

ANSWER KEY - VOCABULARY
Pride and Prejudice

I:1-9	I:10-16	I:17-23	II:1-8	II:9-13	II:14-19
1. D	1. C	1. E	1. B	1. F	1. B
2. F	2. E	2. C	2. E	2. C	2. E
3. A	3. G	3. F	3. D	3. A	3. G
4. E	4. H	4. B	4. F	4. E	4. A
5. H	5. D	5. G	5. C	5. D	5. H
6. B	6. A	6. D	6. A	6. B	6. C
7. I	7. F	7. A			7. F
8. G	8. B				8. D
9. C					

III: 1-5	III:6-10	III:11-19
1. D	1. D	1. C
2. E	2. F	2. F
3. B	3. E	3. H
4. A	4. I	4. G
5. C	5. B	5. D
	6. C	6. E
	7. G	7. B
	8. A	8. A
	9. H	

DAILY LESSONS

LESSON ONE

Objectives
    1. To introduce the *Pride and Prejudice* unit.
    2. To distribute books and other related materials
    3. To preview the study questions for I:1-9
    4. To familiarize students with the vocabulary for I:1-9
    5. To read I:1-9

NOTES: 1. The volume number is in Roman numerals followed by the chapters, so I:1-9 would be Volume I, Chapters 1-9.
            2. Prior to this lesson you need to have told students to bring in pictures (or anything that can be attached to the bulletin board) of things that show either pride or prejudice.

Activity #1

    Have students each explain their pictures--how they relate to pride or prejudice--and let them post their pictures on the bulletin board.

    Explain to the class that the novel they are about to read is a story of pride and prejudice, and alert students to be looking for examples and references to those themes as they read.

Activity #2

    Distribute the materials students will use in this unit. Explain in detail how students are to use these materials.

    Study Guides Students should read the study guide questions for each reading assignment prior to beginning the reading assignment to get a feeling for what events and ideas are important in the section they are about to read. After reading the section, students will (as a class or individually) answer the questions to review the important events and ideas from that section of the book. Students should keep the study guides as study materials for the unit test.

    Vocabulary Prior to reading a reading assignment, students will do vocabulary work related to the section of the book they are about to read. Following the completion of the reading of the book, there will be a vocabulary review of all the words used in the vocabulary assignments. Students should keep their vocabulary work as study materials for the unit test.

    Reading Assignment Sheet You need to fill in the reading assignment sheet to let students know by when their reading has to be completed. You can either write the assignment sheet up on a side blackboard or bulletin board and leave it there for students to see each day, or you can "ditto" copies for each student to have. In either case, you should advise students to become very familiar with the reading assignments so they know what is expected of them.

Extra Activities Center   The Extra Activities page of this unit contains suggestions for an extra library of related books and articles in your classroom as well as crossword and word search puzzles. Make an extra activities center in your room where you will keep these materials for students to use. (Bring the books and articles in from the library and keep several copies of the puzzles on hand.) Explain to students that these materials are available for students to use when they finish reading assignments or other class work early.

Nonfiction Assignment Sheet   Explain to students that they each are to read at least one non-fiction piece from the in-class library at some time during the unit. Students will fill out a nonfiction assignment sheet after completing the reading to help you (the teacher) evaluate their reading experiences and to help the students think about and evaluate their own reading experiences.

Books   Each school has its own rules and regulations regarding student use of school books. Advise students of the procedures that are normal for your school.

Activity #3
Preview the study questions and show students how to do the vocabulary work for I:1-9 of *Pride and Prejudice*. Tell students that they should have this work completed and should complete reading I:1-9 prior to your next class meeting.

NONFICTION ASSIGNMENT SHEET
(To be completed after reading the required nonfiction article)

Name _____ Date _____

Title of Nonfiction Read _____

Written By _____ Publication Date _____

I. Factual Summary: Write a short summary of the piece you read.

II. Vocabulary
    1. With which vocabulary words in the piece did you encounter some degree of difficulty?

    2. How did you resolve your lack of understanding with these words?

III. Interpretation: What was the main point the author wanted you to get from reading his work?

IV. Criticism
    1. With which points of the piece did you agree or find easy to accept? Why?

    2. With which points of the piece did you disagree or find difficult to believe? Why?

V. Personal Response: What do you think about this piece? OR How does this piece influence your ideas?

LESSON TWO

Objectives
1. To review the main ideas and events from I:1-9
2. To preview the study questions and vocabulary for I:10-16
3. To read I:10-16
4. To give students practice reading orally
5. To evaluate students' oral reading

Activity #1

Give students a few minutes to formulate answers for the study guide questions for I:1-9, and then discuss the answers to the questions in detail. Write the answers on the board or overhead transparency so students can have the correct answers for study purposes. NOTE: It is a good practice in public speaking and leadership skills for individual students to take charge of leading the discussions of the study questions. Perhaps a different student could go to the front of the class and lead the discussion each day that the study questions are discussed during this unit. Of course, the teacher should guide the discussion when appropriate and be sure to fill in any gaps the students leave.

Activity #2

Give students about fifteen minutes to preview the study questions for I:10-16 of *Pride and Prejudice* and to do the related vocabulary work.

Activity #3

Have students read I:10-16 of *Pride and Prejudice* out loud in class. You probably know the best way to get readers with your class; pick students at random, ask for volunteers, or use whatever method works best for your group. If you have not yet completed an oral reading evaluation for your students this marking period, this would be a good opportunity to do so. A form is included with this unit for your convenience.

If students do not complete reading I:10-16 in class, they should do so prior to your next class meeting.

ORAL READING EVALUATION - *Pride and Prejudice*

Name _____ Class____ Date _____

SKILL	EXCELLENT	GOOD	AVERAGE	FAIR	POOR
Fluency	5	4	3	2	1
Clarity	5	4	3	2	1
Audibility	5	4	3	2	1
Pronunciation	5	4	3	2	1
_____	5	4	3	2	1
_____	5	4	3	2	1

Total _____   Grade _____

Comments:

LESSON THREE

Objectives
1. To review the main events and ideas from I:10-16
2. To preview the study questions for I:17-23
3. To familiarize students with the vocabulary in I:17-23
4. To read I:17-23

Activity #1
   Give students a few minutes to formulate answers for the study guide questions for I:10-16, and then discuss the answers to the questions in detail. Write the answers on the board or overhead transparency so students can have the correct answers for study purposes.

Activity #2
   Give students about fifteen minutes to preview the study questions for I:17-23 of *Pride and Prejudice* and to do the related vocabulary work.

Activity #3
   Have students read I:17-23 of *Pride and Prejudice* orally in class. Continue the oral reading evaluations.

   If students do not complete reading I:17-23 in class, they should do so prior to your next class meeting.

LESSON FOUR

Objectives
1. To review the main events and ideas from I:17-23
2. To preview the study questions for II:1-8
3. To familiarize students with the vocabulary in II:1-8
4. To read II:1-8

Activity #1
   Give students a few minutes to formulate answers for the study guide questions for I:17-23, and then discuss the answers to the questions in detail. Write the answers on the board or overhead transparency so students can have the correct answers for study purposes.

Activity #2
   Give students the remainder of the class period to do the prereading work for II:1-8 and to read those chapters silently.
   If students do not complete reading II:1-8 in class, they should do so prior to your next class meeting.

LESSON FIVE

Objectives
1. To review the main events and ideas from II:1-8
2. To preview the study questions for II:9-13 and II:14-19
3. To familiarize students with the vocabulary in II:9-13 and II:14-19
4. To read II:9-13 and II:14-19

Activity #1
Give students a few minutes to formulate answers for the study guide questions for II:1-8, and then discuss the answers to the questions in detail. Write the answers on the board or overhead transparency so students can have the correct answers for study purposes.

Activity #2
Give students the remainder of the class period to do the prereading work for II:9-13 and II:14-19 and to read those chapters silently.
Tell students that they are to have this assignment completed by Lesson Seven. (Give students a day and a date.)

LESSON SIX

Objectives
1. To give students the opportunity to practice writing their personal opinions
2. To get students thinking about ways to create successful relationships
3. To give the teacher the opportunity to evaluate students' writing skills

Activity
Distribute Writing Assignment #1. Discuss the directions in detail and give students ample time to complete the assignment.

Follow-Up: After you have graded the assignments, have a writing conference with the students. (This unit schedules one in Lesson Eight.) After the writing conference, allow students to revise their papers using your suggestions and corrections. Give them about three days from the date they receive their papers to complete the revision. I suggest grading the revisions on an A-C-E scale (all revisions well done, some revisions made, few or no revisions made). This will speed your grading time and still give some credit for the students' efforts.

WRITING ASSIGNMENT #1 - *Pride and Prejudice*

PROMPT

Mrs. Bennet is determined to get those girls married off! Finding suitable suitors, though, and getting everyone together *properly* turns out to be quite a challenge.

Your assignment is to write a composition in which you explain what it takes to make a successful relationship with another person.

PREWRITING

Make a list of all the ingredients you think are necessary in a successful relationship. Then go back and number your ingredients in order of importance. Next to each ingredient, jot down a few notes explaining what the ingredient is and a few examples of the ingredient.

DRAFTING

Write an introductory paragraph in which you introduce the idea that certain things are necessary to create a successful relationship.

Write one paragraph for each of the ingredients you have chosen. In each paragraph, state what the ingredient is, explain what you mean, and give a few examples.

Write a paragraph in which you give your final thoughts on the topic and bring your composition to a close.

PROMPT

When you finish the rough draft of your paper, ask a student who sits near you to read it. After reading your rough draft, he/she should tell you what he/she liked best about your work, which parts were difficult to understand, and ways in which your work could be improved. Reread your paper considering your critic's comments and make the corrections you think are necessary.

PROOFREADING

Do a final proofreading of your paper double-checking your grammar, spelling, organization, and the clarity of your ideas.

LESSON SEVEN

Objectives
    1. To check to see that students did the reading assignment
    2. To evaluate students' understanding of the silent reading assignment
    3. To preview the study questions and vocabulary for III:1-5
    4. To read III:1-5

Activity #1

    Quiz - Distribute quizzes and give students about 10 minutes to complete them. (NOTE: The quizzes may either be the short answer study guides or the multiple choice version for II:9-13 and II:14-19.) Have students exchange papers. Grade the quizzes as a class. Collect the papers for recording the grades. (If you used the multiple choice version as a quiz, take a few minutes to discuss the answers for the short answer version if your students are using the short answer version for their study guides.)

Activity #2

    Give students the remainder of the class period to do the prereading work for III:1-5 and to begin the reading assignment. Students should complete reading III:1-5 prior to Lesson Nine. (Give students a day and a date.)

LESSON EIGHT

<u>Objectives</u>
1. To give students the opportunity to practice using the resources of the library
2. To give students some time to work on their nonfiction assignments
3. To give students the opportunity to browse and read about topics that interest them
4. To break up the reading-questions-answers routine

<u>Activity</u>
Take your students to the library. Tell them that the purpose for their being at the library is to find appropriate materials to complete the nonfiction reading assignment that goes along with this unit. Give students ample time to find materials and begin reading.
   Suggested topics:
1. How to make successful relationships
2. Articles of criticism about *Pride and Prejudice*
3. A biography of Jane Austen
4. English history during this period
5. Courtship and marriage in various cultures
6. Effects of divorce on society
7. AIDS and other communicable diseases
8. The consequences of teenage pregnancy
9. The effects of the "sexual revolution" of the 1960's
10. Kinds of prejudice in our society
11. Effects of prejudice
12. Ways to overcome prejudice
13. English gardens
14. Victorian literature
15. Biographical information about rich and influential people in our society

LESSON NINE

Objectives
1. To review the main events and ideas from III:1-5
2. To preview the study questions for III:6-10
3. To familiarize students with the vocabulary in III:6-10
4. To read III:6-10

Activity #1
Give students a few minutes to formulate answers for the study guide questions for III:1-5, and then discuss the answers to the questions in detail. Write the answers on the board or overhead transparency so students can have the correct answers for study purposes.

Activity #2
Give students the remainder of the class period to do the prereading work for III:6-10 and to read those chapters silently. If students do not complete reading III:6-10 in class, they should do so prior to your next class meeting.

LESSON TEN

Objectives
1. To review the main ideas and events of III:6-10
2. To preview the study questions and vocabulary for III:11-19
3. To read III:11-19
4. To widen the breadth of students' knowledge about the topics discussed or touched upon in *Pride and Prejudice*
5. To check students' nonfiction reading assignments

Activity #1
Discuss the answers to the study guide questions for III:6-10. Write the answers on the board for students to copy down for study use later.

Activity #2
Ask each student to give a brief oral report about the nonfiction work he/she read for the nonfiction reading assignment. Your criteria for evaluating this report will vary depending on the level of your students. You may wish for students to give a complete report without using notes of any kind, or you may want students to read directly from a written report, or you may want to do something in between these two extremes. Just make students aware of your criteria in ample time for them to prepare their reports.

Start with one student's report. After that, ask if anyone else in the class has read on a topic related to the first student's report. If no one has, choose another student at random. After each report, be sure to ask if anyone has a report related to the one just completed. That will help keep a continuity during the discussion of the reports.

Activity #3

Tell students that they are to complete the vocabulary work and the reading for III:11-19 prior to Lesson Eleven. (Give students a day and a date.)

LESSON ELEVEN

Objectives
1. To review the main ideas and events from III:11-19
2. To discuss *Pride and Prejudice* on interpretive and critical levels

Activity #1

Take a few minutes at the beginning of the period to review the study questions for III:11-19.

Activity #2

Choose the questions from the Extra Discussion Questions/Writing Assignments which seem most appropriate for your students. A class discussion of these questions is most effective if students have been given the opportunity to formulate answers to the questions prior to the discussion. To this end, you may either have all the students formulate answers to all the questions, divide your class into groups and assign one or more questions to each group, or assign one question to each student in your class. The option you choose will make a difference in the amount of class time needed for this activity.

Activity #3

After students have had ample time to formulate answers to the questions, begin your class discussion of the questions and the ideas presented by the questions. Be sure students take notes during the discussion so they have information to study for the unit test.

EXTRA WRITING ASSIGNMENTS/DISCUSSION QUESTIONS - *Pride and Prejudice*

Interpretation
1. What are the main conflicts in the story, and how are they resolved?
2. In what way is the setting important to the story?
3. From what point(s) of view is the story written?
4. Where is the climax of the story? Justify your answer.
5. Which events in the novel are "turning points"--events which affect the course of the plot?
6. Is there any humor in the story? If so, where. If not, why not?

Critical
7. Compare and contrast the Bennet sisters.
8. Compare and contrast Darcy, Wickham, and Bingley.
9. Compare and contrast Lady De Bourgh, Mrs. Bennet, and Mrs. Gardiner.
10. Is the story of *Pride and Prejudice* believable? Why or why not?
11. Do any of the characters change in the course of the novel? If so, who and how?
12. Are the characters in *Pride and Prejudice* stereotypes? Explain your answer.
13. Compare and contrast the marriages in the novel: Mr. and Mrs. Bennet, Lydia and Wickham, Charlotte Lucas and Mr. Collins, Jane and Bingley, and Elizabeth and Darcy.
14. Explain Caroline Bingley's role in the novel.
15. Compare and contrast Miss De Bourgh and Miss Darcy.
16. Explain the role of pride in the novel.
17. Explain the role of prejudice in the novel.
18. Describe Elizabeth's relationship with Jane.
19. Why did Elizabeth refuse Mr. Collins's marriage proposal?
20. Why did Elizabeth refuse Darcy's proposal, and then why did she later accept it?
21. In what ways is Jane set apart from the other characters in the book?
22. What effect did Lydia's elopement with Wickham have on Lydia, Mrs. Bennet, Mr. Bennet, Elizabeth, and Darcy?
23. What is irony, and how does Jane Austen use it in this novel?

Critical/Personal Response
24. According to Jane Austen, what characteristics are most important for a person to have?
25. According to Jane Austen, what makes a successful marriage/relationship?
26. Suppose Elizabeth had accepted Mr. Collins's proposal? How would that have changed the story and its themes?
27. Characterize Jane Austen's style of writing. How does it contribute to the value of the novel?

Pride and Prejudice Extra Discussion Questions Page 2

<u>Personal Response</u>

28. Would you have liked to have been a part of life in *Pride and Prejudice*? Why or why not?
29. If you could be any of the characters in the book for a short time, which one would you choose? Why?
30. Did you enjoy reading *Pride and Prejudice*? Why or why not?
31. What is pride? Is it good or bad?
32. What is prejudice? How many different kinds of prejudice can you think of? (List them.) Are all prejudices bad?

LESSON TWELVE

Objective
　　To review all of the vocabulary work done in this unit

Activity
　　Choose one (or more) of the vocabulary review activities listed below and spend your class period as directed in the activity. Some of the materials for these review activities are located in the Extra Activities section in this unit.

VOCABULARY REVIEW ACTIVITIES

1. Divide your class into two teams and have an old-fashioned spelling or definition bee.

2. Give each of your students (or students in groups of two, three or four) a *Pride and Prejudice* Vocabulary Word Search Puzzle. The person (group) to find all of the vocabulary words in the puzzle first wins.

3. Give students a *Pride and Prejudice* Vocabulary Word Search Puzzle without the word list. The person or group to find the most vocabulary words in the puzzle wins.

4. Use a *Pride and Prejudice* Vocabulary Crossword Puzzle. Put the puzzle onto a transparency on the overhead projector (so everyone can see it), and do the puzzle together as a class.

5. Give students a *Pride and Prejudice* Vocabulary Matching Worksheet to do.

6. Divide your class into two teams. Use the *Pride and Prejudice* vocabulary words with their letters jumbled as a word list. Student 1 from Team A faces off against Student 1 from Team B. You write the first jumbled word on the board. The first student (1A or 1B) to unscramble the word wins the chance for his/her team to score points. If 1A wins the jumble, go to student 2A and give him/her a definition. He/she must give you the correct spelling of the vocabulary word which fits that definition. If he/she does, Team A scores a point, and you give student 3A a definition for which you expect a correctly spelled matching vocabulary word. Continue giving Team A definitions until some team member makes an incorrect response. An incorrect response sends the game back to the jumbled-word face off, this time with students 2A and 2B. Instead of repeating giving definitions to the first few students of each team, continue with the student after the one who gave the last incorrect response on the team. For example, if Team B wins the jumbled-word face-off, and student 5B gave the last incorrect answer for Team B, you would start this round of definition questions with student 6B, and so on. The team with the most points wins!

7. Have students write a story in which they correctly use as many vocabulary words as possible. Have students read their compositions orally. Post the most original compositions on your bulletin board.

LESSONS THIRTEEN AND FOURTEEN

Objectives
1. To check students' understanding of the characters and events in the novel
2. To give students the opportunity to practice organizing and planning an event
3. To give students the opportunity to work together in small groups
4. To give students the chance to learn about the details of planning a wedding
5 To give students individual writing conferences

Activity #1
Divide your class into groups of three or four students, mixing boys and girls together whenever possible. Distribute the Group Assignments (or write the assignment on the board to conserve paper). Discuss the directions in detail and give students ample time to complete the assignment.

NOTE: If you have the time and inclination, it would be fun to have various students dress and act as the various characters from the novel and to hold a mock wedding for Elizabeth and Darcy.

Activity #2
While students are doing their group work, call individual students to your desk or some other private area where you can hold a writing conference to discuss students' first writing assignments. A Writing Evaluation Form is included for your convenience.

Activity #3
Tell students that they each need to bring in a newspaper account of a wedding for Lesson Fifteen. (Give students the day/date.)

LESSON FIFTEEN

Objectives
1. To give students the opportunity to practice writing to inform
2. To complete the assignment from lessons thirteen and fourteen
3. To give the teacher a chance to evaluate students' individual writing
4. To give students the opportunity to tell each other about the weddings they have planned

Activity #1
Have students exchange newspaper accounts of weddings. They should exchange and read as many as possible in a fifteen-minute time frame. Then discuss the format, style, and contents of the articles.

Activity #2
Distribute Writing Assignment #2. Discuss the directions orally in detail. Allow the remaining class time for students to complete the activity.
If students do not have enough class time to finish, the papers may be collected at the beginning of the next class period.

GROUP ASSIGNMENT - *Pride and Prejudice*

PROMPT

Well, Elizabeth and Darcy finally got engaged! Have you ever noticed that most romance novels end with the couple finally getting engaged--or getting together (and riding off into the sunset!)? Perhaps that's because then the real work begins--starting with the wedding plans. Making the arrangements for a formal wedding takes a great deal of planning. Everything from rings and cake to flowers, gowns and invitations--and scores of other details must be tended to.

ASSIGNMENT

Your assignment is to plan the wedding for Elizabeth and Darcy. Show your knowledge of the characters, choosing things and doing things as you think they would do them.

REQUIREMENTS

Be sure to include at least the following things:
1. The place, time and date
2. The names of those chosen to be in the wedding party
3. A description of the clothing the bride, groom, bridesmaids, and groomsmen will wear
4. A guest list
5. A sample invitation
6. All arrangements relating to the reception--entertainment, food or refreshments, place, decorations, seating arrangements, etc.
7. A description of the decor for the wedding place

Work together as a group to decide on all of these arrangements. Be able to explain how your choices are appropriate. Each group member should write down all arrangements.

WRITING EVALUATION FORM - *Pride and Prejudice*

Name _____ Date _____

Grade _____

Circle One For Each Item:

Grammar:	excellent	good	fair	poor
Spelling:	excellent	good	fair	poor
Punctuation:	excellent	good	fair	poor
Legibility:	excellent	good	fair	poor

Strengths:

Weaknesses:

Comments/Suggestions:

WRITING ASSIGNMENT #2 - *Pride and Prejudice*

PROMPT

You have read several newspaper accounts of weddings and have discussed the elements and style of the articles. Now write a newspaper article for the wedding you planned for Elizabeth and Darcy. Because of Darcy's social position, the article should be more than just a paragraph or two--people will want the nitty-gritty details of the wedding of this wealthy man and his new bride.

PREWRITING

Most of your prewriting has been done during your group work. You have notes about all the details of the wedding; now you just have to organize them and fit them into the newspaper style.

DRAFTING

In the first paragraph of your article, be sure to answer the who, what, when, where, and how questions.

Then, in the body of your article, give the details of the wedding in a logical and complete fashion.

In your concluding paragraph, give any pertinent information regarding the newlyweds' future plans, residence, etc.

PROMPT

When you finish the rough draft of your paper, ask a student who sits near you to read it. After reading your rough draft, he/she should tell you what he/she liked best about your work, which parts were difficult to understand, and ways in which your work could be improved. Reread your paper considering your critic's comments and make the corrections you think are necessary.

PROOFREADING

Do a final proofreading of your paper double-checking your grammar, spelling, organization, and the clarity of your ideas.

LESSON SIXTEEN

Objectives
1. To bring to a culmination the theme of relationships
2. To help give students good, practical, professional advice regarding relationships

Activity
Throughout this unit, students have given some thought to relationships. They have expressed their own opinions and have discussed Jane Austen's ideas and characters.

Invite a marriage counselor to your class to discuss relationships--how to build healthy, strong relationships with other people, pitfalls to avoid, characteristics of successful relationships, characteristics of a successful marriage, etc. Use this class period for the speaker to make his/her presentation and for a question-and-answer session.

LESSON SEVENTEEN

Objectives
1. To give students the opportunity to practice writing to persuade
2. To give the teacher the opportunity to evaluate students' writing skills
3. To further work with the theme of prejudice

Activity #1
Explain to students that they have discussed the idea of prejudice in Jane Austen's novel, and now they will take a look at prejudice in real life today.

Have students give you a definition of prejudice and explain to you why most prejudices are not good. Ask students to offer ways in which prejudice can be overcome.

Have students brainstorm a list of names of characters in books, on television, or in the movies who have definite prejudices. Students should also identify the prejudices the characters have.

Activity #2
Distribute Writing Assignment #3. Discuss the directions in detail and give students ample time to complete the assignment.

LESSON EIGHTEEN

Objective
To review the main ideas presented in *Pride and Prejudice*

Activity #1
Choose one of the review games/activities included in this guide and spend your class period as outlined there. Some materials for these activities are located in the Extra Activities section of this unit.

WRITING ASSIGNMENT #3 - *Pride and Prejudice*

PROMPT

You are familiar with the idea of prejudice--both from our discussions in class and from other sources. You have even given some suggestions as to ways people might be able to overcome prejudice.

Your assignment is to persuade a prejudiced person to give up his/her prejudice. You may either use a fictional character from a book, television show, or movie--or if you know a real-life person who has definite prejudices, you may use that person as your audience. (Change the person's name if you wish.)

PREWRITING

Grab a scratch sheet of paper. On it, write the type of prejudice the person you have chosen has. Jot down a few specific examples of ways that person shows his/her prejudice. Here comes the hard part: write down a few reasons explaining why you think that person is prejudiced. What *causes* the prejudice (in your opinion)? You must think about these things as you create the arguments you are going to use to persuade this person against prejudice. Also put yourself in this person's shoes. What would make *you* change if you were him or her? Considering all these things, write down several arguments to make to persuade this person against prejudice. Next to each argument, write at least one really good, specific example illustrating your point.

DRAFTING

Write your composition as if you were talking to the person you have chosen.

In the first paragraph, write down how you would bring up the subject--what you would say to this person to start your persuasion.

Write one paragraph for each of the arguments you will use. Within each paragraph, state your point, your argument, your reason--and then follow up with at least one specific example to illustrate your point.

After you have made all your points, write a paragraph which would end your "conversation" with this person.

PROMPT

When you finish the rough draft of your paper, ask a student who sits near you to read it. After reading your rough draft, he/she should tell you what he/she liked best about your work, which parts were difficult to understand, and ways in which your work could be improved. Reread your paper considering your critic's comments and make the corrections you think are necessary.

PROOFREADING

Do a final proofreading of your paper double-checking your grammar, spelling, organization, and the clarity of your ideas.

REVIEW GAMES/ACTIVITIES - *Pride and Prejudice*

1. Ask the class to make up a unit test for *Pride and Prejudice*. The test should have 4 sections: matching, true/false, short answer, and essay. Students may use 1/2 period to make the test and then swap papers and use the other 1/2 class period to take a test a classmate has devised (open book). You may want to use the unit test included in this guide or take questions from the students' unit tests to formulate your own test.

2. Take 1/2 period for students to make up true and false questions (including the answers). Collect the papers and divide the class into two teams. Draw a big tick-tack-toe board on the chalk board. Make one team X and one team O. Ask questions to each side, giving each student one turn. If the question is answered correctly, that students' team's letter (X or O) is placed in the box. If the answer is incorrect, no mark is placed in the box. The object is to get three marks in a row like tick-tack-toe. You may want to keep track of the number of games won for each team.

3. Take 1/2 period for students to make up questions (true/false and short answer). Collect the questions. Divide the class into two teams. You'll alternate asking questions to individual members of teams A & B (like in a spelling bee). The question keeps going from A to B until it is correctly answered, then a new question is asked. A correct answer does not allow the team to get another question. Correct answers are +2 points; incorrect answers are -1 point.

4. Have students pair up and quiz each other from their study guides and class notes.

5. Give students a *Pride and Prejudice* crossword puzzle to complete.

6. Divide your class into two teams. Use the *Pride and Prejudice* crossword words with their letters jumbled as a word list. Student 1 from Team A faces off against Student 1 from Team B. You write the first jumbled word on the board. The first student (1A or 1B) to unscramble the word wins the chance for his/her team to score points. If 1A wins the jumble, go to student 2A and give him/her a clue. He/she must give you the correct word which matches that clue. If he/she does, Team A scores a point, and you give student 3A a clue for which you expect another correct response. Continue giving Team A clues until some team member makes an incorrect response. An incorrect response sends the game back to the jumbled-word face off, this time with students 2A and 2B. Instead of repeating giving clues to the first few students of each team, continue with the student after the one who gave the last incorrect response on the team. For example, if Team B wins the jumbled-word face-off, and student 5B gave the last incorrect answer for Team B, you would start this round of clue questions with student 6B, and so on. The team with the most points wins!

UNIT TESTS

SHORT ANSWER UNIT TEST 1 - *Pride and Prejudice*

I. Matching

___ 1. De Bourgh   A. Military man; gambler

___ 2. Jane   B. Darcy's colonel cousin

___ 3. Collins   C. Owner of Pemberly; marries Elizabeth

___ 4. Wickham   D. She warns Elizabeth not to fall in love with Wickham

___ 5. Bingley   E. Bennet home

___ 6. Darcy   F. Lady Catherine

___ 7. Lydia   G. Lady Catherine's home

___ 8. Fitzwilliam   H. She agrees to marry Mr. Collins although she doesn't love him

___ 9. Elizabeth   I. Rich man of Netherfield

___ 10. Charlotte   J. Frank and independent Bennet daughter

___ 11. Gardiner   K. Bingley's place

___ 12. Georgiana   L. Darcy's place

___ 13. Kitty   M. Eldest Bennet daughter; gentle

___ 14. Rosings   N. Younger sister under Lydia's influence

___ 15. Brighton   O. Town where Lydia and Wickham went

___ 16. Netherfield   P. Author

___ 17. Pemberley   Q. Darcy's sister

___ 18. London   R. Lydia is invited by Col. Forster's wife to go there

___ 19. Longbourn   S. Elopes with Wickham

___ 20. Austen   T. Will inherit Longbourn

Pride and Prejudice Short Answer Unit Test 1 Page 2

II. Short Answer

1. Why is Darcy intrigued and attracted by Elizabeth?

2. Although Mrs. Bennet is an unwise and foolish woman, why can we understand her pursuit of rich young men for her daughters?

3. During Darcy and Elizabeth's lively discussion, what character flaws do they attribute to each other?

4. How does Elizabeth's reaction to Wickham's distressing tale differ from Jane's?

5. Why does Darcy's proposal make Elizabeth angry?

Pride and Prejudice Short Answer Unit Test 1 Page 3

6. What does Elizabeth realize about herself after reading Darcy's letter?

7. Do Jane and Elizabeth want to publicize Wickham's character? Why or why not?

8. Why does Elizabeth appeal to her father not to let Lydia go to Brighton?

9. What does Mrs. Gardiner reveal to Elizabeth about Darcy's involvement in Lydia's marriage?

10. What is the result of Lady Catherine's interference?

Pride and Prejudice Short Answer Unit Test 1 Page 4

III. Essay

    Think of another title for *Pride and Prejudice* and explain your choice in detail.

IV. Vocabulary

    Listen to the vocabulary words and write them down. Go back later and write in the correct definitions next to the words.

1.

2.

3.

4.

5.

6.

7.

8.

9.

10.

SHORT ANSWER UNIT TEST 2 - *Pride and Prejudice*

I. Matching

___ 1. De Bourgh   A. Darcy's colonel cousin

___ 2. Jane   B. Bennet home

___ 3. Collins   C. She agrees to marry Mr. Collins although she doesn't love him

___ 4. Wickham   D. Darcy's place

___ 5. Bingley   E. Rich man of Netherfield

___ 6. Darcy   F. Owner of Pemberly; marries Elizabeth

___ 7. Lydia   G. Elopes with Wickham

___ 8. Fitzwilliam   H. Lady Catherine's home

___ 9. Elizabeth   I. Eldest Bennet daughter; gentle

___ 10. Charlotte   J. Lydia is invited by Col. Forster's wife to go there

___ 11. Gardiner   K. Lady Catherine

___ 12. Georgiana   L. Military man; gambler

___ 13. Kitty   M. She warns Elizabeth not to fall in love with Wickham

___ 14. Rosings   N. Darcy's sister

___ 15. Brighton   O. Bingley's place

___ 16. Netherfield   P. Town where Lydia and Wickham went

___ 17. Pemberley   Q. Author

___ 18. London   R. Frank and independent Bennet daughter

___ 19. Longbourn   S. Younger sister under Lydia's influence

___ 20. Austen   T. Will inherit Longbourn

Pride and Prejudice Short Answer Unit Test 2 Page 2

II. Short Answer

1. Describe the personalities of Elizabeth and Jane.

2. Why does Elizabeth dislike Bingley's sisters?

3. What is Mr. Collins' motive for visiting the Bennet family?

4. Describe Elizabeth's double standard concerning Charlotte and Wickham.

5. What kind of a woman is Lady Catherine De Bourgh?

Pride and Prejudice Short Answer Unit Test 2 Page 3

6. Why does Darcy's proposal make Elizabeth angry?

7. What does Elizabeth realize about herself after reading Darcy's letter?

8. Although the elopement is distressing to the family, what gives them cause for greater fear and distress?

9. What does Mrs. Gardiner reveal to Elizabeth about Darcy's involvement in Lydia's marriage?

10. What does Lady Catherine demand of Elizabeth?

Pride and Prejudice Short Answer Unit Test 2 Page 4

III. Composition
1. Compare and contrast Bingley, Darcy, and Wickham.

2. What effect did Lydia's elopement have on the plot and themes of the story?

3. In what ways were "pride" and "prejudice" shown in the novel, and what points were made about those two things?

Pride and Prejudice Short Answer Unit Test 2 Page 5

IV. Vocabulary
   Listen to the vocabulary word and spell it. After you have spelled all the words, go back and write down the definition.

   1.

   2.

   3.

   4.

   5.

   6.

   7.

   8.

   9.

   10.

KEY: SHORT ANSWER UNIT TESTS - *Pride and Prejudice*

The short answer questions are taken directly from the study guides.
If you need to look up the answers, you will find them in the study guide section.

Answers to the composition questions will vary depending on your
class discussions and the level of your students.

For the vocabulary section of the test, choose ten of the
words from the vocabulary lists to read orally for your students.

The answers to the matching section of the test are below.

Answers to the matching section of the Advanced Short Answer Unit Test
are the same as for Short Answer Unit Test #2.

<u>Test #1</u>
1. F
2. M
3. T
4. A
5. I
6. C
7. S
8. B
9. J
10. H
11. D
12. Q
13. N
14. G
15. R
16. K
17. L
18. O
19. E
20. P

<u>Test #2</u>
1. K
2. I
3. T
4. L
5. E
6. F
7. G
8. A
9. R
10. C
11. M
12. N
13. S
14. H
15. J
16. O
17. D
18. P
19. B
20. Q

ADVANCED SHORT ANSWER UNIT TEST - *Pride and Prejudice*

I. Matching

___ 1. De Bourgh   A. Darcy's colonel cousin

___ 2. Jane   B. Bennet home

___ 3. Collins   C. She agrees to marry Mr. Collins although she doesn't love him

___ 4. Wickham   D. Darcy's place

___ 5. Bingley   E. Rich man of Netherfield

___ 6. Darcy   F. Owner of Pemberley; marries Elizabeth

___ 7. Lydia   G. Elopes with Wickham

___ 8. Fitzwilliam   H. Lady Catherine's home

___ 9. Elizabeth   I. Eldest Bennet daughter; gentle

___ 10. Charlotte   J. Lydia is invited by Col. Forster's wife to go there

___ 11. Gardiner   K. Lady Catherine

___ 12. Georgiana   L. Military man; gambler

___ 13. Kitty   M. She warns Elizabeth not to fall in love with Wickham

___ 14. Rosings   N. Darcy's sister

___ 15. Brighton   O. Bingley's place

___ 16. Netherfield   P. Town where Lydia and Wickham went

___ 17. Pemberley   Q. Author

___ 18. London   R. Frank and independent Bennet daughter

___ 19. Longbourn   S. Younger sister under Lydia's influence

___ 20. Austen   T. Will inherit Longbourn

Pride and Prejudice Advanced Short Answer Unit Test Page 2

II. Short Answer
1. Compare and contrast the Bennet sisters.

2. Compare and contrast Darcy, Wickham, and Bingley.

3. Compare and contrast Lady De Bourgh, Mrs. Bennet, and Mrs. Gardiner.

Pride and Prejudice Advanced Short Answer Unit Test Page 3

4. Compare and contrast the marriages in the novel: Mr. and Mrs. Bennet, Lydia and Wickham, Charlotte Lucas and Mr. Collins, Jane and Bingley, and Elizabeth and Darcy.

5. Explain the role of pride in the novel.

6. Explain the role of prejudice in the novel.

Pride and Prejudice Advanced Short Answer Unit Test Page 4

III. Essay

Elizabeth says, "There are few people whom I really love, and still fewer of whom I think well. The more I see of the world, the more I am dissatisfied with it; and every day confirms my belief of the inconsistency of all human characters, and of the little dependence that can be placed on the appearance of either merit or sense."
Knowing the people in Elizabeth's world and the events that took place there, explain why she makes this statement. Use specific examples from the book.

Pride and Prejudice Advanced Short Answer Unit Test Page 5

IV. Vocabulary

   Listen to the vocabulary words and write them down. After you have written down all the words, write a paragraph using all of the vocabulary words. The paragraph must in some way relate to *Pride and Prejudice*.

MULTIPLE CHOICE UNIT TEST 1 - *Pride and Prejudice*

I. Matching

___ 1. De Bourgh   A. Military man; gambler

___ 2. Jane   B. Darcy's colonel cousin

___ 3. Collins   C. Owner of Pemberley; marries Elizabeth

___ 4. Wickham   D. She warns Elizabeth not to fall in love with Wickham

___ 5. Bingley   E. Bennet home

___ 6. Darcy   F. Lady Catherine

___ 7. Lydia   G. Lady Catherine's home

___ 8. Fitzwilliam   H. She agrees to marry Mr. Collins although she doesn't love him

___ 9. Elizabeth   I. Rich man of Netherfield

___ 10. Charlotte   J. Frank and independent Bennet daughter

___ 11. Gardiner   K. Bingley's place

___ 12. Georgiana   L. Darcy's place

___ 13. Kitty   M. Eldest Bennet daughter; gentle

___ 14. Rosings   N. Younger sister under Lydia's influence

___ 15. Brighton   O. Town where Lydia and Wickham went

___ 16. Netherfield   P. Author

___ 17. Pemberley   Q. Darcy's sister

___ 18. London   R. Lydia is invited by Col. Forster's wife to go there

___ 19. Longbourn   S. Elopes with Wickham

___ 20. Austen   T. Will inherit Longbourn

Pride and Prejudice Multiple Choice Unit Test 1 Page 2

II. Multiple Choice

1. How does Mr. Darcy conduct himself at the ball?
    A. He is flirtatious with all of the ladies.
    B. He is proud and formal and makes no effort to get to know anyone.
    C. He is shy and spends most of his time walking in the garden.
    D. He is loud and boisterous and makes improper remarks; no one likes him.

2. True or False: Charlotte excuses Darcy by saying that he has a lot to be proud of--money, family connections, and good looks.
    A. True
    B. False

3. What opinion does Charlotte have that she shares with Elizabeth?
    A. She says that Darcy is not to be trusted, and will bring sorrow to any woman who becomes involved with him.
    B. She says that Jane should make her feelings about Mr. Bingley known, or he may think her indifferent and become attracted to someone else.
    C. She says Jane is far too outspoken.
    D. She says Mrs. Bennet should be less reserved in expressing her opinions.

4. What is Mr. Collins' motive for visiting the Bennet family?
    A. He wants to check on Mr. Bennet's health.
    B. He wants to look over the estate since he is already planning to sell it when Mr. Bennet dies.
    C. He wants to choose a wife from among the Bennet sisters.
    D. He wants to withdraw his claim on the estate and leave it to Bennet's daughters.

5. How does Mr. Collins react to Miss Bennet's rejection of his marriage proposal?
    A. He is insulted and threatens to throw the family out of the house if she does not accept.
    B. He thinks she is doing it to be flirtatious. It is beyond his comprehension to think he would be rejected.
    C. He desperately wants to get married, so he offers to keep all of the other sisters in the house until they get married. He also offers to let Mrs. Bennet live there as long as she wishes.
    D. He cheerfully reminds her that she has four sisters, and one of them will be smart enough to marry him. He also insinuates that she will not be welcome in the house after he is the owner.

Pride and Prejudice Multiple Choice Unit Test 1 Page 3

6. Which of the following does *not* describe Lady Catherine De Bourgh?
    A. She is very rich.
    B. She is full of pride and self-importance.
    C. She is used to getting her own way in everything with little or no debate.
    D. She is very lavish in the gifts she gives to those she likes.

7. What does Elizabeth realize after reading Darcy's letter?
    A. She realizes that Wickham was going to take advantage of her.
    B. She realizes that Darcy really is as snobbish and ill-tempered as she originally suspected.
    C. She realizes that she placed her trust on Wickham's good looks and easy sociability, forgetting completely about the impropriety of his disclosures and actions.
    D. She realizes that she is tired of thinking about men and about relationships in general. She decides she needs a rest.

8. Why does Mr. Bennet allow Lydia to go ahead with her plans to go to Brighton?
    A. He is stubborn: he is doing it simply because the others are against it, and he wants to assert himself as head of the family.
    B. He is tired of Lydia's complaining and wants to get rid of her for a while.
    C. She is his favorite daughter, and he will do anything she asks.
    D. He believes that when she is exposed to a place with a larger number of ladies, she will realize her own insignificance.

9. Elizabeth finds many things about her father's behavior "reprehensible." Which of the following is *not* one of her objections?
    A. He married solely on the basis of physical attraction and engaging personality.
    B. He ridicules his wife to amuse himself.
    C. He spends too much time reading, instead of seeing to the affairs of the family.
    D. He has been negligent in seeing that his daughters are brought up properly.

10. What does Elizabeth think of Georgianna?
    A. She thinks Georgianna is a snob like the others.
    B. She thinks Georgianna is shy and not as proud as she had supposed.
    C. She thinks Georgianna is just plain mean.
    D. She thinks Georgianna is much smarter than the others and a worthy friend.

Pride and Prejudice Multiple Choice Unit Test 1 Page 4

11. What does Lady Catherine demand of Elizabeth?
    A. She demands that Elizabeth go to school and get a proper education so that she can be a better wife.
    B. She demands that Elizabeth travel around the continent for two years before she settles down.
    C. She demands that Elizabeth never agree to marry Darcy.
    D. She demands that Elizabeth allow her first-born daughter to be raised by Lady Catherine so that she is "brought up properly."

12. What is the result of Lady Catherine's interference?
    A. She unknowingly gives Darcy hope that Elizabeth thinks better of him than she used to.
    B. She drives an insurmountable wedge between Elizabeth and Darcy.
    C. She loses Darcy's respect and affection. He says he will never speak to her again.
    D. She creates a firm friendship between her daughter and Elizabeth.

Pride and Prejudice Multiple Choice Unit Test 1 Page 5

III. Composition
    Write ONE of the following letters:
    a. A letter from Elizabeth to Darcy after she reads his letter which explains his actions she has criticized.
    b. A letter from Miss Bingley to a friend about Elizabeth's coming to visit Jane while she is sick at Netherfield.
    c. A letter from Lady Catherine to Darcy after her unsuccessful visit with Elizabeth.
    d. A letter from Darcy to Wickham after his elopement with Lydia.
    e. A letter from Mrs. Gardiner to Mrs. Bennet after her trip to Pemberley.

Pride and Prejudice Multiple Choice Unit Test 1 Page 6

IV. Vocabulary   Multiple choice. Write in the letter of the word that matches the definition.

    ____ 1. CAPRICE   A. Showing regret or remorse

    ____ 2. VAGUE   B. Judgement; wisdom

    ____ 3. VALID   C. Of little significance

    ____ 4. REQUITED   D. Manageable; easily handled

    ____ 5. ASPIRE   E. Hesitate as a result of conscience

    ____ 6. CONJUGAL   F. Advanced; chased after

    ____ 7. TRACTABLE   G. Cheerful willingness

    ____ 8. OMEN   H. Money given to support the clergy

    ____ 9. ENGROSSED   I. Repaid

    ____ 10. PURSUED   J. Desire; to have as an ambition or a goal

    ____ 11. ASCERTAINING K. Unclear; not well-defined

    ____ 12. SCRUPLE   L. Legal and binding

    ____ 13. IMPERTINENT   M. Improperly bold or forward

    ____ 14. SAGACITY   N. Added

    ____ 15. EFFICACY   O. Totally occupied

    ____ 16. PENITENT   P. Relating to marriage

    ____ 17. AUGMENTED   Q. Effectiveness

    ____ 18. ALACRITY   R. Discovering

    ____ 19. TITHES   S. A prophetic sign

    ____ 20. TRIFLING   T. Impulsive change of mind

MULTIPLE CHOICE UNIT TEST 2 - *Pride and Prejudice*

I. Matching

___ 1. De Bourgh A. Darcy's colonel cousin

___ 2. Jane B. Bennet home

___ 3. Collins C. She agrees to marry Mr. Collins although she doesn't love him

___ 4. Wickham D. Darcy's place

___ 5. Bingley E. Rich man of Netherfield

___ 6. Darcy F. Owner of Pemberley; marries Elizabeth

___ 7. Lydia G. Elopes with Wickham

___ 8. Fitzwilliam H. Lady Catherine's home

___ 9. Elizabeth I. Eldest Bennet daughter; gentle

___ 10. Charlotte J. Lydia is invited by Col. Forster's wife to go there

___ 11. Gardiner K. Lady Catherine

___ 12. Georgiana L. Military man; gambler

___ 13. Kitty M. She warns Elizabeth not to fall in love with Wickham

___ 14. Rosings N. Darcy's sister

___ 15. Brighton O. Bingley's place

___ 16. Netherfield P. Town where Lydia and Wickham went

___ 17. Pemberley Q. Author

___ 18. London R. Frank and independent Bennet daughter

___ 19. Longbourn S. Younger sister under Lydia's influence

___ 20. Austen T. Will inherit Longbourn

Pride and Prejudice Multiple Choice Unit Test 2 Page 2

II. Multiple Choice

1. How does Mr. Darcy conduct himself at the ball?
    A. He is shy and spends most of his time walking in the garden.
    B. He is loud and boisterous and makes improper remarks; no one likes him.
    C. He is proud and formal and makes no effort to get to know anyone.
    D. He is flirtatious with all of the ladies.

2. True or False: Charlotte excuses Darcy by saying that he has a lot to be proud of--money, family connections, and good looks.
    A. True
    B. False

3. What opinion does Charlotte have that she shares with Elizabeth?
    A. She says Mrs. Bennet should be less reserved in expressing her opinions.
    B. She says Jane is far too outspoken.
    C. She says that Darcy is not to be trusted and will bring sorrow to any woman who becomes involved with him.
    D. She says that Jane should make her feelings about Mr. Bingley known, or he may think her indifferent and become attracted to someone else.

4. What is Mr. Collins' motive for visiting the Bennet family?
    A. He wants to choose a wife from among the Bennet sisters.
    B. He wants to withdraw his claim on the estate and leave it to Bennet's daughters.
    C. He wants to check on Mr. Bennet's health.
    D. He wants to look over the estate since he is already planning to sell it when Mr. Bennet dies.

5. How does Mr. Collins react to Miss Bennet's rejection of his marriage proposal?
    A. He cheerfully reminds her that she has four sisters, and one of them will be smart enough to marry him. He also insinuates that she will not be welcome in the house after he is the owner.
    B. He desperately wants to get married, so he offers to keep all of the other sisters in the house until they get married. He also offers to let Mrs. Bennet live there as long as she wishes.
    C. He thinks she is doing it to be flirtatious. It is beyond his comprehension to think he would be rejected.
    D. He is insulted and threatens to throw the family out of the house if she does not accept.

Pride and Prejudice Multiple Choice Unit Test 2 Page 3

6. Which of the following does *not* describe Lady Catherine De Bourgh?
    A. She is very lavish in the gifts she gives to those she likes.
    B. She is very rich.
    C. She is full of pride and self-importance.
    D. She is used to getting her own way in everything with little or no debate.

7. What does Elizabeth realize after reading Darcy's letter?
    A. She realizes that Darcy really is as snobbish and ill-tempered as she originally suspected.
    B. She realizes that she placed her trust on Wickham's good looks and easy sociability, forgetting completely about the impropriety of his disclosures and actions.
    C. She realizes that Wickham was going to take advantage of her.
    D. She realizes that she is tired of thinking about men and about relationships in general. She decides she needs a rest.

8. Why does Mr. Bennet allow Lydia to go ahead with her plans to go to Brighton?
    A. He believes that when she is exposed to a place with a larger number of ladies, she will realize her own insignificance.
    B. He is tired of Lydia's complaining and wants to get rid of her for a while.
    C. She is his favorite daughter, and he will do anything she asks.
    D. He is stubborn: he is doing it simply because the others are against it and he wants to assert himself as head of the family.

9. Elizabeth finds many things about her father's behavior "reprehensible." Which of the following is *not* one of her objections?
    A. He spends too much time reading, instead of seeing to the affairs of the family.
    B. He has been negligent in seeing that his daughters are brought up properly.
    C. He married solely on the basis of physical attraction and engaging personality.
    D. He ridicules his wife to amuse himself.

10. What does Elizabeth think of Georgianna?
    A. She thinks Georgianna is just plain mean.
    B. She thinks Georgianna is much smarter than the others and a worthy friend.
    C. She thinks Georgianna is a snob like the others.
    D. She thinks Georgianna is shy and not as proud as she had supposed.

Pride and Prejudice Multiple Choice Unit Test 2 Page 4

11. What does Lady Catherine demand of Elizabeth?
    A. She demands that Elizabeth allow her first-born daughter to be raised by Lady Catherine so that she is "brought up properly."
    B. She demands that Elizabeth go to school and get a proper education so that she can be a better wife.
    C. She demands that Elizabeth travel around the continent for two years before she settles down.
    D. She demands that Elizabeth never agree to marry Darcy.

12. What is the result of Lady Catherine's interference?
    A. She drives an insurmountable wedge between Elizabeth and Darcy.
    B. She loses Darcy's respect and affection. He says he will never speak to her again.
    C. She creates a firm friendship between her daughter and Elizabeth.
    D. She unknowingly gives Darcy hope that Elizabeth thinks better of him than she used to.

Pride and Prejudice Multiple Choice Unit Test 2 Page 5

III. Composition

Explain and defend ONE of these two statements made by Mark Schorer, who wrote the introduction to an edition of *Pride and Prejudice*:

Every character, however entertaining in himself, however important to the mechanical plot, has a further function; every character is in some important way integrated in the theme of the novel, so that the novel presents us with a various and, finally, exact dramatic analysis of that theme.

The novel is a comic and complex study of self-importance and egotism and malice as these are absorbed from a society whose morality and values are derived from the economics of class; a study, further, in the mitigation of these traits as the hero and heroine come into self-recognition, as their individual beings rise momentarily above that society and then sink back into it again.

Pride and Prejudice Multiple Choice Unit Test 2 Page 6

III. Vocabulary

____ 1. DESTITUTE	A. Manageable; easily handled

____ 2. PENITENT	B. Praise; compliment

____ 3. TRIFLING	C. Cheerful willingness

____ 4. TITHES	D. Improperly bold or forward

____ 5. INCUMBENT	E. Insulting; disrespectful; rude

____ 6. COGENT	F. Showing regret or remorse

____ 7. CIRCUMSPECTION	G. Unclear; not well-defined

____ 8. ALACRITY	H. Convincing

____ 9. QUERULOUS	I. Implied by action

____ 10. OBLIGE	J. Imposed as a duty or obligation

____ 11. INSOLENT	K. Pleas

____ 12. IMPLACABLE	L. Of little significance

____ 13. PANEGYRIC	M. Not talkative

____ 14. TACIT	N. Grumbling; complaining

____ 15. ENTREATIES	O. Prudence

____ 16. VAGUE	P. Impossible to appease or please

____ 17. PURSUED	Q. Advanced; chased after

____ 18. IMPERTINENT	R. Do a favor or service for

____ 19. TRACTABLE	S. Money given to support the clergy

____ 20. TACITURN	T. Lacking; poor

ANSWER SHEET - *Pride and Prejudice*
Multiple Choice Unit Tests

I. Matching	II. Multiple Choice	IV. Vocabulary
1. ___	1. ___	1. ___
2. ___	2. ___	2. ___
3. ___	3. ___	3. ___
4. ___	4. ___	4. ___
5. ___	5. ___	5. ___
6. ___	6. ___	6. ___
7. ___	7. ___	7. ___
8. ___	8. ___	8. ___
9. ___	9. ___	9. ___
10. ___	10. ___	10. ___
11. ___	11. ___	11. ___
12. ___	12. ___	12. ___
13. ___		13. ___
14. ___		14. ___
15. ___		15. ___
16. ___		16. ___
17. ___		17. ___
18. ___		18. ___
19. ___		19. ___
20. ___		20. ___

ANSWER KEY - *Pride and Prejudice*
Multiple Choice Unit Tests

Answers to Unit Test 1 are in the left column. Answers to Unit Test 2 are in the right column.

I. Matching	II. Multiple Choice	IV. Vocabulary
1. F K	1. B C	1. T T
2. M I	2. A A	2. K F
3. T T	3. B D	3. L L
4. A L	4. C A	4. I S
5. I E	5. B C	5. J J
6. C F	6. D A	6. P H
7. S G	7. C B	7. D O
8. B A	8. D A	8. S C
9. J R	9. C A	9. O N
10. H C	10. B D	10. F R
11. D M	11. C D	11. R E
12. Q N	12. A D	12. E P
13. N S		13. M B
14. G H		14. B I
15. R J		15. Q K
16. K O		16. A G
17. L D		17. N Q
18. O P		18. G D
19. E B		19. H A
20. P Q		20. C M

UNIT RESOURCE MATERIALS

BULLETIN BOARD IDEAS - *Pride and Prejudice*

1. Save one corner of the board for the best of students' *Pride and Prejudice* writing assignments.

2. Take a word search puzzle from the extra activities section and with a marker copy it over in a large size on the bulletin board. Write the clue words to find to one side. Invite students prior to and after class to find the words and circle them on the bulletin board.

3. Title the board *Pride and Prejudice*: A NOVEL FULL OF CHARACTERS. Find pictures in magazines (or perhaps your library has a file of pictures) of people who look like the various characters in the novel. Place the picture on colorful paper, write the character's name under the picture (or next to it), and write a brief description of the character by it. You may wish to arrange these pictures on a genealogical table to show the relationships among the characters.

4. Title the board PRIDE AND PREJUDICE. As an introductory activity (see Lesson One), have students bring in pictures which show examples of pride or prejudice in our society. Have each student explain his/her picture and post it on the bulletin board.

5. Title the board PRIDE AND PREJUDICE. Make a "house" on the board for each of the home places in the book (Netherfield, Longbourn, Meryton, Rosings, Hunsford, and Pemberley). Place the names of the characters associated with each place within the appropriate "house" to help students get the names and places straight as they begin to read the book.

6. Write several of the most significant quotations from the book onto the board on brightly colored paper.

7. Make a bulletin board listing the vocabulary words for this unit. As you complete sections of the novel and discuss the vocabulary for each section, write the definitions on the bulletin board. (If your board is one students face frequently, it will help them learn the words.)

8. Make a "social ladder" of the characters in the book, showing the relationships among them.

9. Do a bulletin board about etiquette, giving tips about manners and appropriate behavior from Miss Manners or some such person.

EXTRA ACTIVITIES

One of the difficulties in teaching a novel is that all students don't read at the same speed. One student who likes to read may take the book home and finish it in a day or two. Sometimes a few students finish the in-class assignments early. The problem, then, is finding suitable extra activities for students.

The best thing I've found is to keep a little library in the classroom. For this unit on *Pride and Prejudice,* a biography of Jane Austen would be interesting for some students. You can include other related books and articles about courtship and marriage, formal English gardens, English military service during the period, etiquette, Victorian literature, or critics' articles about *Pride and Prejudice.*

Other things you may keep on hand are puzzles. We have made some relating directly to *Pride and Prejudice* for you. Feel free to duplicate them.

Some students may like to draw. You might devise a contest or allow some extra-credit grade for students who draw characters or scenes from *Pride and Prejudice.* Note, too, that if the students do not want to keep their drawings you may pick up some extra bulletin board materials this way. If you have a contest and you supply the prize (a CD or something like that perhaps), you could, possibly, make the drawing itself a non-refundable entry fee.

The pages which follow contain games, puzzles and worksheets. The keys, when appropriate, immediately follow the puzzle or worksheet. There are two main groups of activities: one group for the unit; that is, generally relating to the *Pride and Prejudice* text, and another group of activities related strictly to the *Pride and Prejudice* vocabulary.

Directions for these games, puzzles and worksheets are self-explanatory. The object here is to provide you with extra materials you may use in any way you choose.

MORE ACTIVITIES - *Pride and Prejudice*

1. Pick a chapter or scene with a great deal of dialogue and have the students act it out on a stage. (Perhaps you could assign various scenes to different groups of students so more than one scene could be acted and more students could participate.)

2. Use some of the related topics (noted earlier for an in-class library) as topics for research, reports or written papers, or as topics for guest speakers.

3. Have students keep a journal of their reactions to and thoughts about the characters. They should make an entry for each character after each reading assignment. When they finish reading the novel, they should reread all of their entries to see how (if at all) their opinions of the characters changed.

4. Take short scenes from the novel. Assign parts in the scenes to various students (so that each student has a part). Students should memorize their lines and dress up as their characters to perform their scenes in front of the class in your classroom or on stage.

5. Have students design a book cover (front and back and inside flaps) for *Pride and Prejudice*.

6. Have students design a bulletin board (ready to be put up; not just sketched) for *Pride and Prejudice*.

7. Hold a class discussion comparing and contrasting etiquette today with etiquette 100 years ago.

8. In a class discussion, compare and contrast the principles set forth in *Pride and Prejudice* with the principles of our society today. Try to get students to vocalize what changes there have been and how they came about. (Consider, for example, the Bennets' problem of Lydia's reputation.)

9. Show a film version of *Pride and Prejudice*. Have students compare and contrast the film with the book and voice their opinions about how the film was alike or different from the way they pictured the people and events in their own minds as they read.

WORD SEARCH - *Pride and Prejudice*

All words in this list are associated with *Pride and Prejudice*. The words are placed backwards, forward, diagonally, up and down. The included words are listed below the word searches.

```
L D L Y N V C B B Y B X Q W K V H W C L L Y Y D
M K C C T W R D V H F N B A B D N K K K N J L Q
V V R Y R X C N C I Q J P Z P T V W J G Y E Q T
L G X M X Z Q K T R K Y B S K P S G N B I H R B
T F C V G F K Z H L C R H N W W E B Q F D J Y Q
C H Y A J S W B V N I X C N V X S A R K B X Z V
H O J P R I D F M G G Q D Y S R S E R K G J R X
W E L M L R B G H P P B H A E Y H B B A E J B X
W G C L N N I T K P G Y H T R T V D S A N G R M
D D I N I J O A V E R M T S E C T E L L L C B Z
V A I D A N A I G R O E G N P A Y O C R Y L E W
M N U N O D S A T E L N J H G E U N L E O D P S
W M E D E W I R R A I K T U N S H S L R I W I H
J R N W N R I E G S T E I O D G N G T R A V Q A
K O B T R V N C O K B U M T R I N O P E N H P R
L B R A D I D R K A N B P U T I C L T E N L C S
D J M N D N X J Z H C K O E B Y N E D E E N S N
C J G R T Q K I J Z A B F J R P F R S H K P R M
H G A K J B L F R F E M V L K C A T Z S P N H Z
M G H G G E X S V D X D Y Y K G W B G K V P S N
```

APPEARANCES	DEBOURGH	JEALOUS	PAY
AUSTEN	DINE	KITTY	PREJUDICE
BALL	ELIZABETH	LETTERS	PRIDE
BINGLEY	EYES	LONDON	REPUTATION
BRIGHTON	FITZWILLIAM	LYDIA	ROSINGS
CARRIAGE	GARDEN	MARRIAGE	WICKHAM
CHARLOTTE	GARDINER	MONEY	WORLD
COLLINS	GEORGIANA	MUD	
DANCE	HELP	NETHERFIELD	
DARCY	JANE	NOTE	

CROSSWORD - *Pride and Prejudice*

CROSSWORD CLUES - *Pride and Prejudice*

ACROSS

1. Lydia is invited by Col. Forster's wife to go there
4. Will inherit Longbourn
6. The more I see of the ___ the more I am dissatisfied with it
8. What things seem to be
12. Younger sister under Lydia's influence
13. Speak
14. Elopes with Wickham
15. Dine
17. One does this at a ball
18. Elizabeth arrived at Netherfield covered in it
22. Eat dinner
23. Abbreviation for colonel
24. A place to take walks
25. Short letter
29. Present plural of to be
30. Means of communication
32. ___ and Prejudice
33. Town where Lydia and Wickham went
34. The way a story closes
35. Pride and ___

DOWN

1. A kind of event where there is dancing
2. Present singular of to be
3. Darcy ___ed the Bennets; aided
4. She agrees to marry Mr Collins although she doesn't love him
5. Negative reply
6. Military man; gambler
7. Means of transportation
8. Author
9. Darcy had to --- Wickham's debts
10. Frank and independent Bennet daughter
11. Elizabeth's attracted Darcy
16. Lady Catherine ___
19. Owner of Pemberley
20. Rich man of Netherfield
21. Darcy's sister
24. She warns Elizabeth not to fall in love with Wickham
26. Eldest Bennet daughter; gentle
27. Clothing; what people wear
28. Miss Bingley is ___ that Elizabeth has Darcy's interest
31. Darcy had lots of it; he was rich

CROSSWORD ANSWER KEY - *Pride and Prejudice*

MATCHING QUIZ/WORKSHEET 1 - *Pride and Prejudice*

____ 1. NOTE   A. Elopes with Wickham

____ 2. PAY   B. Lydia is invited by Col. Forster's wife to go there

____ 3. DEBOURGH   C. Darcy's pleasant cousin; colonel

____ 4. JANE   D. Elizabeth's attracted Darcy

____ 5. MONEY   E. Eat dinner

____ 6. DINE   F. A kind of event where there is dancing

____ 7. EYES   G. Rich man of Netherfield

____ 8. BALL   H. Lady Catherine ___

____ 9. BINGLEY   I. Owner of Pemberley

____ 10. CARRIAGE   J. Means of communication

____ 11. LYDIA   K. Short letter

____ 12. DANCE   L. The Bennets were concerned about Lydia's _____

____ 13. WICKHAM   M. Darcy had to --- Wickham's debts

____ 14. LETTERS   N. The more I see of the ___ the more I am dissatisfied with it

____ 15. HELP   O. Means of transportation

____ 16. DARCY   P. Eldest Bennet daughter; gentle

____ 17. BRIGHTON   Q. Military man; gambler

____ 18. REPUTATION   R. Darcy had lots of it; he was rich

____ 19. FITZWILLIAM   S. One does this at a ball

____ 20. WORLD   T. Darcy ____ed the Bennets; aided

MATCHING QUIZ/WORKSHEET 2 - *Pride and Prejudice*

____ 1. ROSINGS   A. A place to take walks

____ 2. DINE   B. Miss Bingley is ___ that Elizabeth has Darcy's interest

____ 3. LYDIA   C. One does this at a ball

____ 4. JEALOUS   D. Lady Catherine's home

____ 5. DARCY   E. What things seem to be

____ 6. BRIGHTON   F. Elopes with Wickham

____ 7. PAY   G. A kind of event where there is dancing

____ 8. COLLINS   H. The more I see of the ___ the more I am dissatisfied with it

____ 9. MUD   I. Owner of Pemberley

____ 10. PRIDE   J. Rich man of Netherfield

____ 11. APPEARANCES   K. Town where Lydia and Wickham went

____ 12. BALL   L. ___ and Prejudice

____ 13. DANCE   M. Frank and independent Bennet daughter

____ 14. CARRIAGE   N. Elizabeth arrived at Netherfield covered in it

____ 15. BINGLEY   O. Means of transportation

____ 16. GARDEN   P. Lydia is invited by Col. Forster's wife to go there

____ 17. ELIZABETH   Q. Will inherit Longbourn

____ 18. LONDON   R. Eat dinner

____ 19. WORLD   S. Darcy had to ___ Wickham's debts

____ 20. DEBOURGH   T. Lady Catherine ___

KEY: MATCHING QUIZ/WORKSHEETS - *Pride and Prejudice*

Worksheet 1	Worksheet 2
1. K	1. D
2. M	2. R
3. H	3. F
4. P	4. B
5. R	5. I
6. E	6. P
7. D	7. S
8. F	8. Q
9. G	9. N
10. O	10. L
11. A	11. E
12. S	12. G
13. Q	13. C
14. J	14. O
15. T	15. J
16. I	16. A
17. B	17. M
18. L	18. K
19. C	19. H
20. N	20. T

JUGGLE LETTER REVIEW GAME CLUE SHEET - *Pride and Prejudice*

SCRAMBLED	WORD	CLUE
UBHREDOG	DEBOURGH	Lady Catherine ___
NEAJ	JANE	Eldest Bennet daughter; gentle
LOSNILC	COLLINS	Will inherit Longbourn
MACHKIW	WICKHAM	Military man; gambler
YINGELB	BINGLEY	Rich man of Netherfield
CARDY	DARCY	Owner of Pemberley
YADIL	LYDIA	Elopes with Wickham
ALZETBEHI	ELIZABETH	Frank and independent Bennet daughter
WLAFZLTIMII	FITZWILLIAM	Darcy's pleasant cousin; colonel
RETDEIFLHNE	NETHERFIELD	Mrs. Bennet wants Eliz. & Jane to stay overnight at ___ Hall
RAGAMEIR	MARRIAGE	Mr. Collins disregards Elizabeth's rejection of his ___ proposal
TOTEHALRC	CHARLOTTE	She agrees to marry Mr. Collins though she doesn't love him
DOLRW	WORLD	The more I see of the ___ the more I am dissatisfied with it
RRDINEGA	GARDINER	She warns Elizabeth not to fall in love with Wickham
THINGOBR	BRIGHTON	Lydia is invited by Col. Forster's wife to go there
ANAGGROIE	GEORGIANA	Darcy's sister
OSLUJAE	JEALOUS	Miss Bingley is ___ that Elizabeth has Darcy's interest
PLEH	HELP	Darcy ___ed the Bennets; aided
NOODLN	LONDON	Town where Lydia and Wickham went
LABL	BALL	A kind of event where there is dancing
SGINISOR	ROSINGS	Lady Catherine's home
USANTE	AUSTEN	Author
SEEY	EYES	Elizabeth's attracted Darcy
PRAECSENAPA	APPEARANCES	What things seem to be
DUM	MUD	Elizabeth arrived at Netherfield covered in it
NIDE	DINE	Eat dinner
AYP	PAY	Darcy had to --- Wickham's debts
TIKTY	KITTY	Younger sister under Lydia's influence
RAGEIARC	CARRIAGE	Means of transportation
CANDE	DANCE	One does this at a ball
REETSTL	LETTERS	Means of communication
DRIPE	PRIDE	___ and Prejudice
TONE	NOTE	Short letter
RUJCIDEEP	PREJUDICE	Pride and ___
PEUNATOIRT	REPUTATION	The Bennets were concerned about Lydia's ___
NOEMY	MONEY	Darcy Had lots of it; he was rich
NARGED	GARDEN	A place to take walks

VOCABULARY RESOURCE MATERIALS

VOCABULARY WORD SEARCH - *Pride and Prejudice*

All words in this list are associated with *Pride and Prejudice* with an emphasis on the vocabulary words chosen for study in the text. The words are placed backwards, forward, diagonally, up and down. The included words are listed below.

```
T Z D S T T N Q L Q F I Q J P A N E G Y R I C Y
D A Y I V Q V H S A J H M R S T E N L X N V C S
R E C T I T U D E U G A V P R O F L I G A T E F
D A Q I X L E E Z H Y U I N R Y A J P L L H M V
T D D K T T C V R E O R J K V U N Y I U T Y T M
P B Q I I U V O G U E B E N T Y D D N I R E H B
N M R U L M R I G C L S E E O E F E T A N C Q R
R B Q E G A L N I E P O P I R C M Y N I W V S J
F E A B V B T R Q O N R U I S O S E U C V R C N
R A D F O I P O C N E T S S T A C G N I E O F J
I Q S M F A T K R P G I M N T R N O N I N S I V
V M X T C I V Y Q Y O B E S E A I C X J P N C D
A E P L I A N C Y N D T C M S S U F E T V E Y V
C L R L F D T I H Z I E C N U M B C L E N C R L
I Q A A A P I J T N K B F F B K T M C I A Q D W
J M N C C C W O E Y M G F E D U D T F C N V Q T
R H P Q R I A P U X P E N X R D I K I M F G Q W
C D B U R I T B R S F T Y E Y V L F T C Z G Y W
K C N S T D T Y L M B W W T E T F B S L F M P B
P U R S U E D Y Y E B N M S D E T N E M G U A B
```

AFFINITY	DILATORY	OBEISANCE	REQUITED
ALACRITY	ECSTASY	OBLIGE	SANGUINE
ASPIRE	EFFICACY	OMEN	SCRUPLE
AUGMENTED	EFFUSION	PANEGYRIC	TACIT
BREVITY	ENVY	PENITENT	TACITURN
CAPRICE	FASTIDIOUS	PERPETUALLY	TITHES
COGENT	IMPLACABLE	PLIANCY	TRIFLING
CONJECTURE	IMPRUDENCE	PROFLIGATE	VAGUE
CONJUGAL	IMPUTE	PURSUED	VALID
COPSE	INCUMBENT	QUERULOUS	VERACITY
DEFER	INVECTIVES	RECTITUDE	VOGUE
DERISION	MERCENARY	REPINE	VOID

VOCABULARY CROSSWORD - *Pride and Prejudice*

VOCABULARY CROSSWORD CLUES - *Pride and Prejudice*

ACROSS
1. Opposite of bad
2. Discovering
6. Fashion; popularity
9. Postpone
10. A kind of event where there is dancing
11. Spat; lovers' petty quarrel
12. Eat dinner
13. Impulsive change of mind
16. Meticulous; difficult to please
20. The one after
21. Anger
22. Writing instrument
24. Wreck
25. Unclear; not well-defined
27. Fortunate
29. Have a feeling of discontent aroused by a desire for the possessions or qualities of others
31. Present plural of to be
33. Implied by action
34. Thicket of small trees
35. Short letter
36. Empty
38. To be discontented or in low spirits
41. Darcy had to --- Wickham's debts
42. Ridicule
43. Credit
45. Coordinating conjunction
46. No one could --- Mrs. Bennet (please; gratify)
47. ___ and Prejudice

DOWN
1. A place to take walks
2. A natural attraction to
3. Prudence
4. Desire; to have as an ambition or a goal
5. Negative reply
6. Legal and binding
7. Acquire
8. Unrestrained outpouring of speech
9. Lacking; poor
14. Flexibility
15. Effectiveness
17. Haughty; disdainful
18. Impossible to appease or please
19. Characteristic of making unwise decisions
23. A prophetic sign
25. Truthfulness
26. Money given to support the clergy
28. Favorable
29. Pleas
30. Fluency of speech
32. Quality of being short in duration; shortness
33. Not talkative
37. Convincing
39. Elizabeth's attracted Darcy
40. Darcy ____ed the Bennets; aided
44. Elizabeth arrived at Netherfield covered in it

VOCABULARY CROSSWORD - *Pride and Prejudice*

VOCABULARY WORKSHEET 1 - *Pride and Prejudice*

____ 1. Postpone
    A. Trifling   B. Aspire   C. Cogent   D. Defer

____ 2. Empty
    A. Aspire   B. Valid   C. Requited   D. Void

____ 3. Quality of being short in duration; shortness
    A. Brevity   B. Tacit   C. Circumspection   D. Void

____ 4. Flexibility
    A. Supercilious   B. Brevity   C. Pliancy   D. Volubility

____ 5. Of little significance
    A. Trifling   B. Propitious   C. Ascertaining   D. Defer

____ 6. Money given to support the clergy
    A. Brevity   B. Tithes   C. Perpetually   D. Incumbent

____ 7. Totally occupied
    A. Engrossed   B. Effusion   C. Fastidious   D. Conjecture

____ 8. A gesture of deference or homage
    A. Taciturn   B. Destitute   C. Oblige   D. Obeisance

____ 9. Hesitate as a result of conscience
    A. Scruple   B. Copse   C. Impertinent   D. Sanguine

____ 10. Impulsive change of mind
    A. Ecstasy   B. Profligate   C. Impute   D. Caprice

____ 11. Unclear; not well-defined
    A. Perpetually   B. Vague   C. Repine   D. Profligate

____ 12. Continually; constantly
    A. Volubility   B. Efficacy   C. Effusion   D. Perpetually

____ 13. Credit
    A. Veracity   B. Copse   C. Vague   D. Impute

____ 14. Showing regret or remorse
    A. Penitent   B. Brevity   C. Oblige   D. Caprice

____ 15. Discovering
    A. Ascertaining   B. Requited   C. Dilatory   D. Impute

____ 16. Manageable; easily handled
    A. Profligate   B. Sagacity   C. Impertinent   D. Tractable

____ 17. Ridicule
    A. Derision   B. Taciturn   C. Engrossed   D. Scruple

____ 18. Legal and binding
    A. Pursued   B. Implacable   C. Valid   D. Omen

____ 19. Moral uprightness
    A. Mercenary   B. Vague   C. Trifling   D. Rectitude

____ 20. Impossible to appease or please
    A. Implacable   B. Querulous   C. Dilatory   D. Scruple

VOCABULARY WORKSHEET 2 - *Pride and Prejudice*

____ 1. VOLUBILITY   A. Repaid

____ 2. VAGUE   B. Impossible to appease or please

____ 3. ASCERTAINING   C. A prophetic sign

____ 4. REQUITED   D. Pleas

____ 5. FASTIDIOUS   E. Fluency of speech

____ 6. IMPUTE   F. Credit

____ 7. EFFUSION   G. Unrestrained outpouring of speech

____ 8. IMPLACABLE   H. Meticulous; difficult to please

____ 9. COGENT   I. Haughty; disdainful

____ 10. ENTREATIES   J. Added

____ 11. VOID   K. Discovering

____ 12. INVECTIVES   L. Fashion; popularity

____ 13. REPINE   M. Empty

____ 14. VOGUE   N. Truthfulness

____ 15. TRIFLING   O. To be discontented or in low spirits

____ 16. AUGMENTED   P. Unclear; not well-defined

____ 17. VERACITY   Q. Abusive language

____ 18. SUPERCILIOUS   R. Convincing

____ 19. OMEN   S. Ridicule

____ 20. DERISION   T. Of little significance

KEY: VOCABULARY WORKSHEETS - *Pride and Prejudice*

Worksheet 1	Worksheet 2
1. D	1. E
2. D	2. P
3. A	3. K
4. C	4. A
5. A	5. H
6. B	6. F
7. A	7. G
8. D	8. B
9. A	9. R
10. D	10. D
11. B	11. M
12. D	12. Q
13. D	13. O
14. A	14. L
15. A	15. T
16. D	16. J
17. A	17. N
18. C	18. I
19. D	19. C
20. A	20. S

VOCABULARY JUGGLE LETTER REVIEW GAME CLUES - *Pride and Prejudice*

SCRAMBLED	WORD	CLUE
RACICPE	CAPRICE	Impulsive change of mind
MPCNOUETRCSICI	CIRCUMSPECTION	Prudence
ESTGNAIRACNI	ASCERTAINING	Discovering
OTFSUDIIAS	FASTIDIOUS	Meticulous; difficult to please
YALCIPN	PLIANCY	Flexibility
EIUSRCPSULIO	SUPERCILIOUS	Haughty; disdainful
UOGEV	VOGUE	Fashion; popularity
YFNAFTII	AFFINITY	A natural attraction to
CFIYCEFA	EFFICACY	Effectiveness
ALYCTAIR	ALACRITY	Cheerful willingness
BLIMPALEAC	IMPLACABLE	Impossible to appease or please
TEDTUITES	DESTITUTE	Lacking; poor
FAYAILTIBF	AFFABILITY	Quality of being pleasant & easy to speak with
ETRSTAINEE	ENTREATIES	Pleas
UNDERECMIP	IMPRUDENCE	Characteristic of making unwise decisions
SNTOENIL	INSOLENT	Insulting; disrespectful; rude
TOOSRUPPII	PROPITIOUS	Favorable
RYICAVET	VERACITY	Truthfulness
TANRUCTI	TACITURN	Not talkative
MUNNTEBIC	INCUMBENT	Imposed as a duty or obligation
STIETH	TITHES	Money given to support the clergy
FONFESUI	EFFUSION	Unrestrained outpouring of speech
JUTEECCRON	CONJECTURE	Guess
TDUETECIR	RECTITUDE	Moral uprightness
PUMETI	IMPUTE	Credit
PEERIN	REPINE	To be discontented or in low spirits
NAYEECRRM	MERCENARY	Motivated by money or material goods
NSOOITSUTTEA	OSTENTATIOUS	Pretentious; pompous
RUSDEUP	PURSUED	Advanced; chased after
GOSDENSER	ENGROSSED	Totally occupied
TENRIMTNEPI	IMPERTINENT	Improperly bold or forward
CABLERTAT	TRACTABLE	Manageable; easily handled
RIONSEDI	DERISION	Ridicule
RULCSEP	SCRUPLE	Hesitate as a result of conscience
NUCYPERAI	PECUNIARY	Relating to money
PETNENIT	PENITENT	Showing regret or remorse

SEACENBOI	OBEISANCE	A gesture of deference or homage
MIIIUTNOND	DIMINUTION	Reduction
EASYCST	ECSTASY	Intense joy
BUVYTIILLO	VOLUBILITY	Fluency of speech
JUTSONNICNI	INJUNCTIONS	Commands; orders
NGUOJLAC	CONJUGAL	Relating to marriage
EUOSULRUQ	QUERULOUS	Grumbling; complaining
BRAPNATOOPI	APPROBATION	Approval
LRIGNTIF	TRIFLING	Of little significance
TERIVYB	BREVITY	Quality of being short in duration; shortness
GOLTREAIPF	PROFLIGATE	Wasteful; extravagant
GNASIENU	SANGUINE	Cheerfully confident; optimistic
CVIEVTSEIN	INVECTIVES	Abusive language
ALYORDIT	DILATORY	Tending to delay
MUGDEENAT	AUGMENTED	Added
FEERD	DEFER	Postpone
SEPOC	COPSE	Thicket of small trees
QTDUEIER	REQUITED	Repaid
LADVI	VALID	Legal and binding
ENYV	ENVY	Have a feeling of discontent aroused by a desire for the possessions or qualities of others
GETNOC	COGENT	Convincing
EGVAU	VAGUE	Unclear; not well-defined
YLLEEPPUTRA	PERPETUALLY	Continually; constantly
BEIGOL	OBLIGE	Do a favor or service for
RYAGCPENI	PANEGYRIC	Praise; compliment
REPAIS	ASPIRE	Desire; to have as an ambition or a goal
ATTIC	TACIT	Implied by action
TYAGICSA	SAGACITY	Judgement; wisdom
DOIV	VOID	Empty
NOME	OMEN	A prophetic sign

www.ingramcontent.com/pod-product-compliance
Lightning Source LLC
Chambersburg PA
CBHW080037100526
44584CB00023BA/3405